T0328348

# Team Killers

# Team Killers

A Comparative Study of Collaborative Criminals

Jennifer Furio

Algora Publishing
New York

Algora Publishing, New York
© 2001 by Algora Publishing
All rights reserved. Published 2001.
Printed in the United States of America
Editors@algora.com

Soft cover ISBN: 1-892941-62-7
Hard cover ISBN: 1-892941-63-5

Library of Congress Cataloging-in-Publication Data 2001-004086

Furio, Jennifer.
  Team killers / by Jennifer Furio.
    p. cm.
  1. Team murder—Case studies. 2. Team murderers—Case studies. I.
Title.
  HV6515 .F87 2001
  364.15'23—dc21
                                        2001004086

# Table of Contents

We absolutely must do more to fathom the criminal mind by seeing its participation in our common humanity. Early in my life (pre-teens, in fact) I decided that I had to harbor inside me every possible human impulse I could think of to feel, powerfully feel, my links with that spectrum of humanity. Not to BECOME a murderer, of course, but to explore within me the impulses to become one. . . I have frightened and nauseated myself in my attempts to "know" rather than simply "hate." This has shaped the entirety both of my personhood and my writing career.

Leonard Berkman
*Author and Professor*
*Chairman of Drama and Theater, Smith College*

Assigning Responsibility in Collaborative Killings

All humans are social creatures, but when two or more people collaborate in the most feared and taboo of criminal acts — killing — questions are raised that go beyond standard or "commonsense" understandings of sociability.

The Law falls short when it comes to delimiting culpability in the realm of homicide, where social and moral issues must be taken into account. How do we define homicide? Once, the distinction between first- and second-degree murder involved a fairly clear difference between a clear and considered determination to kill another person, versus a sudden impulse to kill during a moment of conflict or stress. It has now collapsed into a vague attempt to distinguish between a decision to kill that is taken (as many states define it) "in a moment in time, however brief," and a decision to kill that is taken without that "moment in time, however brief." What is a jury to make of this? The difference is considerable, and can lead to sentences ranging from a mere twenty years to life imprisonment without parole.

The definition of manslaughter is similarly slippery: a homicide where no intent need be proved, only recklessness or negligence on the part of the perpetrator. That leaves the door open to a host of fine moral distinctions, which the defense attorneys are happy to guide us in examining.

Beyond this, there is the matter of justified or excused homicide, where the person who has been killed was acknowledged as being wicked, or attempted to perpetrate great harm on an innocent person. Self defense and the defense of others is another fertile field for public debate.

A commonsense definition of homicide is that it involves the intention to terminate the life of a specific person. In some cases, where the motive is material gain (as in insurance or robbery cases), this definition seems adequate. But, commonsense also assumes that human beings are rational creatures, and most murders make no sense at all if judged by the model of a rational person's intentions. Intentionally killing, for no reason beyond passionate hatred, jealousy, or uncontrollable anger, seems inconsistent with the notion of rational behavior.

This commonsense model of rational human action fails because *it presumes a much greater degree of social detachment* than actually can be found throughout the population. We commonly think of the "individual" as a person who has private goals, relating to his own preferences, and who pursues his life with the intention of achieving these goals, while interacting with a throng of similarly self-interested individuals. The inimitable Mrs. Thatcher is quoted as saying, "There is no such thing as society, only persons." Sociability is considered secondary, a proclivity for others that one may exercise in any degree that one finds comfortable, considering that the individually-held objectives come first. In this rationalistic model of individualism, the law exists to intimidate the individual into conformity, by making a plausible threat that violation will be excessively costly, depriving the individual of the things that s/he really wants. Violation of the law, then, would be a miscalculation, presuming the crime were detected.

Another aspect of this commonsense individualism emphasizes the idea that sometimes "emotions" may overcome reason and lead to a crime of passion. The law makes some minor allowance for this, but only when a jury of commonsense persons can find that, if they were in the same situation as the accused, they too would be likely to act irrationally. The most extreme form of this is to be found in the insanity defense, which has become so thoroughly muddied by constant efforts to refine just what counts as insanity that it is virtually useless. If the individual is sane enough to stand trial, he is considered sane enough to be found guilty. Thus, the law relies on a general assumption that individuals are rational and calculating.

But what about those situations where a homicide is committed by more than one person?

Suppose one accepts that humans are not just sociable by choice, but may be irremediably caught up in social relationships over which they often have no control whatsoever. In that case, involvement in even a homicide may be the consequence of the social bond, more than of any individually chosen course of action.

Social relationships are not often between equals; and the degree and force of the inequality can vary greatly. At the most benign end of the spectrum, two persons may have the sort of deep friendship that is sometimes called male bonding. If one of them becomes involved in a situation that moves toward homicide, the other may help — simply out of loyalty. The most extreme form of this can be found among soldiers, who frequently bond so closely that they will help each other in truly atrocious murders. Long after the event, the participants may remember what they did with intense shame and remorse.

Spouses may join forces to commit a homicide, the one (usually the woman) not really wishing to kill but feeling pulled in by her spouse's involvement. In cases of this sort, the person who went along with and helped in the killing may be able to articulate very clear feelings of remorse at what s/he recognizes as a terribly wrong act.

The common thread of this sort of collaborative killing is the recognition by *some* of the actors that the deed was really wrong. They have a "standard" social conscience, and may be able to articulate the intense feelings of loyalty that overwhelmed that conscience. Loyalty is a major element of a "normal" social life; its overriding effect could hardly excuse the participant, but it is worth noting that an excess of a desirable trait usually seems less wicked than the absence of anything positive in the motives of the accused.

When the social relationship between the participants in a collaborative killing is less equal, the apportionment of blame, at least in the form of an indictment, often takes little account of that situation. If an older and more experienced person effectively plays on the insecurities of a younger associate, boasting of the crimes he has ruthlessly committed and, in effect, challenging the younger person to "prove himself," he has engaged in a perversion of the rites of passage. In extreme cases, the older person may have achieved such an aura of power that he can tell an underling to commit a murder and expect to be obeyed without having to involve himself directly in carrying out the deed. The resultant crime may appear to be the work of the "fall guy" underling, who usually will not "roll over" and implicate the boss; but it is certainly the latter's work at least as much as his own. In a crime organization, one moves up by proving himself to be a "hard man," ready to do whatever he is told without qualms or questions.

The intense emotional dependence that arises within an abusive relationship between man and woman (or, occasionally, in same-sex relationships) can create what appears to be a similar dynamic, but there are important differences involved.

The central dynamic of an abusive relationship is the abused person's inability to escape the cycle of alternating abuse and reconciliation. An abuser who never lets up is not likely to succeed; what is needed is abuse, then cessation — often with a false reconciliation. The extension of love, followed by withdrawal and estrangement, appears to work powerfully on the victim, depriving her/him of the ability to flee, but, even more strongly, creating a pathological desire to please. The victim descends into a state of utter dependency, which the abuser often exploits cunningly in carrying out criminal plans.

Abused persons do not make good killers, but they can be employed in a variety of ways that involve them in a homicidal situation. They may become accomplices by driving a car used in a felony that turns out to involve a murder, or help lure a victim to his death, or assist in kidnapping someone who dies as a result of the crime. Getting rid of a body or covering up other evidence is not full complicity in a murder; however, if it is done with prior knowledge that a homicide is contemplated, then it does count as aid. A cynical or assiduous prosecutor can often find ways of trapping the person into making a statement implying prior knowledge — and that is enough to allow the jury a "reasonable inference" of full complicity.

Recruitment scenarios can also lure an individual into participating in an activity that turns homicidal. Often, there is an unexpressed but clear threat for failure to comply and, equally, there may be little or no description of anything more that what is required of the recruit. In such cases, the actual subcultural milieu in which this takes place is a crucial factor in evaluating the real character of the threat. Someone living on the "mean streets," where threat is omnipresent and escape is virtually unthinkable, may be under brutal social pressures quite unthinkable to the jury, the prosecutor or the judge. The law allows a plea of duress; but the members of the court may not be in a position to assess whether duress existed. Extreme social pressures should, reasonably, take into account that for many people it is virtually unimaginable to leave behind the place that they know, for once and for all — even if that is the only alternative to complying with a command to involve oneself in a crime. Our laws say only that duress is an excuse if one is threatened by imminent death or great bodily harm; but that defense cannot be used in murder cases, even those special felony murder cases where the individual went along with a criminal act that turned out to involve a murder.

Children must be judged according to a different model altogether. Overwhelming social pressure is clearly at play in cases where a child is enlisted in a criminal act that results in death. In common law, a child below the age of eight is deemed not capable of committing a crime, whereas one between eight and twelve is presumed incapable unless the prosecution can prove otherwise. Above the age of twelve, the presumption is that the child understands the gravity of a crime, especially murder. What has been overlooked is the matter of justifiable homicide and the tendency of a child to take other people's judgments as definitive.

We live in a culture in which nearly every child is saturated with the sight of homicides, justifiable and unjustifiable, on a daily basis. Televised representations generally make a clear distinction between homicides committed by villains and the necessary and entirely justifiable killing of those same rogues; but the question of what makes a rogue is terrifyingly simplified. Rogues are people who harm or threaten the persons or property of the *Good*. Unobjectionable enough — but this lays a trap for the child's mind.

Children who benefit from anything resembling a normal upbringing are intensely loyal to their primary group. It is from this group — first parents, then peers — that they get their sense of who the *Good* are. The child doesn't think in terms of an abstract concept of a good person: innocent, law abiding, harmless; the child thinks in terms of "mine" and "others." If "my" people say the "others" are bad, then everything the child has learned supports him in thinking that it is right and good to treat the others harshly, even to the point of killing them.

Death itself is an alien concept to the young. The false, tidy villain-killing portrayed in the entertainment media gives no hint of the terrible social rupture caused by (almost) anyone's death. Child killers, brought into court to see the anguish of those who loved their victim, are often reduced to tears at their first hint of what death really means to the living. It follows, then, that children far beyond the age of twelve who are recruited into a homicidal adventure cannot know what a person of even thirty can know of its meaning. When we combine that ignorance with the intense bond of group loyalty, it is no surprise that children can participate in terrible killings.

In a similar way, the socially isolated can easily be manipulated by their desperate need for social acceptance. Camus' Mersault, feeling his estrangement from the normal bonds of society, was an easy mark for the man who befriended him only in order to recruit an accomplice to murder. So, at both ends of the spectrum of social attachment and estrangement, there are powerful social impulses that can lead people to participate in killing.

War is a state-sponsored example. Young people are recruited under threat, taught the art of killing, told who the "enemy" are and compelled to participate in the most awful of collaborative killings. Where the state, rather than the situation, defines friend and enemy, it takes on the exact moral character of a mastermind in the killing of not one or a few, but perhaps millions. All of the arts of social pressure, solicited loyalty, bonding, threat, and defining the enemy are consciously practiced.

The most coercive cults can also lead to murder. The appeal of a cult is that it provides the socially excluded with an intensely attractive illusion — social acceptance with a simulacrum of love and esteem. All that is required is that the individual surrender any private moral conscience to the dictates of the group, as manipulated by its leadership. Cults, inherently morally revisionist, promise redemption to the dispossessed. Unusual activities may be portrayed as spiritual practices, which the followers understand to be the guarantee that they will never again be alone. The followers accept the premise that the leader(s) have a deep wisdom and understanding, offering something pure and fine in place of the shallow and false morality of everyday life (which excluded them, and which the cult members now reject). Outsiders gradually become villains. And the villains are no trifling matter — they are, in fact, the authors of the great social pathology of the world outside the cult. Thus, their death hardly seems deplorable. Indeed death, even for the members themselves, can come to be seen as an attractive adventure — for "religion" can offer the promise of a perfect and endless life once one has rejected (or been rejected from) the mortal coil of everydayness.

Is this an exercise in spinning excuses for a whole category of criminals, or an attempt to offer a slew of loopholes through which killers can slip to evade just punishment? The best I can say is that projects like Jennifer Furio's books are undertaken to make the public aware that crimes of this sort have their roots in the sociability of humankind, to remove the strangeness, the alien quality so often attributed to them by uncomprehending people.

Determining the exact degree of culpability and thus what punishment is appropriate are matters for careful consideration; no "one-size-fits-all" approach can suffice. In 1787, the English philosopher William Godwin said that, one day, society would attach no more moral blame to the killer than to the knife he used. We may never see that day, but we may come finally to place the killer within society and see his (or her) crime as something more than a wayward action taken by an individual propelled by inexplicable drives.

*J. W. Premiston, PhD*
Professor of Jurisprudence, Penal Systems and Crime
Eastern Washington University

Studying Team Killers

Murders committed by people working in teams are just as gruesome as those committed by killers who work alone — or even worse. As some of the examples in this book make plain, it can be just as chancy to accept a ride offered by a couple as it is to hop into a car driven by a single male. And, while we may like to assume that women are nurturers, their participation in such crimes often heightens the cruelty and sadism.

Building on the topics that are explored in my previous books, *The Serial Killer Letters: A Penetrating Look Inside the Minds of Murderers*, and *Voices from Prison: Letters from Women Murderers*, I have set out to examine the terrifying phenomenon of people who form a partnership and commit murder, and who then go on to commit more murders until they get caught. Simply stated, couples or groups that kill are most often found to be made up of individuals who have degenerate tendencies, but it is only when they come together that their combined personality becomes lethal. The French have coined the expression *folie à deux* to indicate a delusion shared by two emotionally-linked persons. Is the organized whole greater than the sum of its parts, here as in so many other social forms of activity? It seems that it is.

Usually the duo is involved in a sexual relationship, "enhanced" by the murders, though sometimes they have a more ordinary purpose. Often, a variety of complicated rationales are at play: some teams kill as part of other crimes, for money, or they may be driven by political passions or prejudice and hatred. There are variations within the culture of serial murderers that kill in couples. Within the pages of this book, all the principal types of groups will be examined.

When I began this project, I believed — based on my study of passive-aggressive relationships — that I would be analyzing men, principally, and the women who help them kill. Instead, I found that dominance was the key factor in the making of any killing team, whatever the gender of the partners. The group or couple originates around the more powerful model's ability to persuade, induce, coerce, or terrorize another into joining his or her nefarious game. To assume that these couples are always made up of male leaders who victimize women, and who are solely responsible for the crimes, is wrong.

In *all* the teams, one dominant member orchestrates the activities and relies on a submissive, easily-manipulated partner to assist. Usually, a man takes that role — statistics show that men dominate almost every team-killing couple. However, there are male/male teams, and female/female teams — in which case, one woman is dominant and takes on the lethal leadership role. The leader may be more active in carrying out the murders, or may organize the event without actually "bloodying his or her own hands"; either way, one person is in control. This brings up the question of patterns of submissive mates, and the dangers of passive/aggressive dynamics, regardless of gender.

So we must create definitive categories, and look at the differences between the various types of killing teams; but all the while we must understand that the common thread weaving between the couples, whatever their make up, is a dominant character. We will examine gender's role in this dynamic, but keep our focus on the factor of dominance.

Sometimes it doesn't take much for the leader to create a "killing machine" in his or her partner; a willing mate, at the least suggestion, may become equally titillated and active in initiating the killing. Jealousy and fear of losing a lover are sometimes overwhelming motivators. Other times, the leader turns up the pressure so that passion and romance turn into passion and thrill, then passion and coercion, and then, finally, terror.

The leaders' ability to manipulate their partners into doing something they would not have done alone reflects a common "talent" found in individual serial killers: to find and exploit another person's weaknesses. This talent helps them trap their prey, and their partners as well. And once a leader has a partner, he or she is ready to go out, search for and hunt down prey, and act out what usually turn out to be control-related fantasies of possession and "termination."

I know this to be true from clinical and academic literature — and I also know it personally. In the course of my correspondence and telephone conversations with numerous serial killers, male and female, I have come to recognize various tactics they utilize to dominate others — the various ways they introduce even a journalist to their powerful, larger-than-life personalities. When a serial killer decides someone may be useful, whether as a writer or a possible "player" or victim, he takes off the mask of normalcy and reveals a power to con, to ignite fear, to create submission on a level rarely encountered outside this world of deviancy.

After pondering this reality and the fact that few readers (I hope) will have my own up-close-and-personal perspective, I decided that, while this book should focus on the dynamics of team serial killers, I should also share with you something of my own experience by weaving in a few telling excerpts from my journals, and the recurring images that now haunt me.

Many readers of my first book wondered *why* I had spoken to killers in any event, and why they had decided to talk to me. I believe it is only because I made a conscious decision that the information they could provide would outweigh my own sensitivity or personal difficulty in dealing with the subjects; I was willing to overlook my own discomfort in order to obtain a wealth of information from these people directly. In *Letters from Prison: Voices of Women Murderers*, I went further and included excerpts from my own letters, so that the reader would have a better understanding of the process. As a result, I was able to offer a glimpse into violent minds, and two books of fresh material to be interpreted.

Taking the next step, in *Team Killers* I wish not only to explore this subculture of violent killers, but to offer some stories along the way about what an author experiences while gathering information from killers. Don't get me wrong: it isn't always ugly. Then again, it is at times overwhelming, especially given that these heinous murders should have been avoidable.

People still question me regularly about my own interactions with these criminals — the bonding, fear, and guilt that inevitably result from recognizing the individual self — for better or worse — of those whom we prefer to consider maniacal. As bizarre as the subjects and my relationships with them may seem, beyond their monikers and the commercial hype that has surrounded them, I did become aware of and, in some cases, come to understand their rage. Never to condone it, but to understand it at some level. I have cried during an execution. Conversely, I have also developed a compulsion to double-check the deadbolts on my doors. I have shared thoughts and feelings with killers, and I have become the focus of their calculated attention — so that I have a sense of just how the serial killer may have smiled, and persuaded a woman to go with him.

During television interviews, I sometimes find that comparisons are drawn to *Dead Man Walking, The Silence of the Lambs* or *Hannibal Lecter*. I am not Susan Sarandon, a nun counseling inmates; nor am I interested in promoting the unrealistic views promulgated by such commercial entertainment. Still, I have noted some parallels between real life and some of these movie versions of the woman with a "killer relationship." And so while tabloid versions of real life tragedy are mockeries, it would be inappropriate not to address those parallels.

People are naturally curious about why I have chosen to write about this specific topic, and about what that experience has brought me. I have felt revelation, an increased sense of self, a purpose and power after facing the darkness that can inhabit the human mind and soul; equally, I realize that at times I've placed myself in a precarious position. I have sensed that I was toying with my own emotional stability and physical health. I can say, however, that at the end of the day, on some level, I'm a step closer to recognizing the many factors that create killers.

I have developed more respect for our judicial system, although there are many ways in which it needs to be improved. The system appears to be overwhelmed by an epidemic, and those responsible for upholding the law and protecting the citizens are desperately trying to hold back the tide. Our antiquated system is unable to handle juvenile killers, lust killers, and team killers; the role of mental illness is inadequately represented; and our ability to ascertain responsibility and assign guilt is insufficient.

As I was writing this book, the tragic Yates drowning occurred in Texas — five children were drowned by their mother. Five children died. As horrible as the circumstances were, the husband had compassion for his wife and wished to understand her, rather than send her off to the executioner. The jury wanted information about magnified states of postpartum depression. But a year ago, when a similar tragedy occurred, the mother/killer was executed. Within just months, even the most punitive states are realizing that that was one more death that brought the country no closer to a solution. The children are still buried. It appears that our society is beginning to understand that, although Mrs. Yates did kill her children, executing her might not be the answer. In fact, there might be something to learn from the heartbreak. We seem to be starting to give precedence to the grave need for fundamental change — which can only be based on a more thorough understanding of the different natures of various crimes. And with a more thorough understanding, we may, someday, reduce or prevent such unspeakable acts.

Anguish of various kinds has driven individuals to "snap" and commit one-time murders of one or more victims. By contrast, the kind of team-perpetrated murders considered in this book are not spontaneous but are planned and calculated, so that they represent an even more appalling distortion of humanity's capabilities. While most of these repeated crimes are driven by sexual deviancy, it would be misleading to suggest that that is always a component. Some people kill out of a need to feel power; others kill to serve their own political agenda. Legally, morally, these are surely not acceptable rationales for murder, any more than sex would be.

By the same token, it would be hypocritical to defend the death penalty. If persons are allowed to kill for any reason, individually or collectively, we create a society based on barbarism. The ACLU pointed out in a study completed in 1999* that victims' fam-

---

*ACLU News Wire, Civil Liberties in the News, 1999, Internet Edition, "The Death Penalty and Victims' Families."

ily members are *more* depressed when the persons who killed their loved ones are executed. The reasons are twofold: one, they have lost the target for their anger, and two, in 87% of the cases, the event is anti-climactic and leaves the victim's family confused and depressed. When humans take each other's life, is any one purpose somehow more justified than another? In my view, even after speaking with murderers, and with families of those who have been murdered, the answer is simply "no."

Serial killers (as individuals) tend to be male, aged 30s to 40s, and usually of low to average intelligence, capable holding of a menial job. Many are married, many are white. In this book, we are introduced to an entirely new subset of the "culture" of serial killers: those who not only set out to kill, time after time, but who recruit partners to work with them. At times, the introduction is personal, since I have come to know many of these persons through my research.

The cases that follow are not limited to the United States. Team killing is not an isolated phenomenon. And since a very high percentage of murder cases are never solved, we cannot even gauge how widespread it is.

# PART I
## MALE/FEMALE TEAMS

Most killing teams are comprised of one heterosexual man and one woman; this category, being the largest, can be broken down into sub-types for closer examination.

Specific evidence tells us something about the profile of the "typical" female team killer. She works in cooperation with a man. They are usually sexual partners, and their killings are mostly sexual in nature. According to the available statistics, the female in a serial killing team is younger than "autonomous" female serial murderers: most often, she becomes tied to her male counterpart in her early twenties. She is vulnerable at this age, easily manageable for her partner. And the victims are younger still, ranging between the ages of nine and fifteen, on average.

The murderous duo can only loosely be defined as "organized" in their activities — the female's jealousy and ambivalence in participating in her predator-partner's games can lead to poor planning, sloppiness in hiding the evidence, and so on.

In most cases, the male controls the female's actions more than she does herself. Her age, coupled with the manipulative character- istics of the male serial killer, leave her highly suggestible — a pup- pet, of sorts. To some degree, she becomes willing to overcome her inherently monogamous nature in deference to her man. As long as she is part of the sexual fantasy, she feels less threatened by his need to bring other women into their "union" to fulfill himself. As the crimes begin to escalate, the female killer becomes more systematic, more organized in the planning of the murders. She derives pleasure from the power she feels within the relationship when he praises her. Is she a "happy" woman? Is his approval enough to alleviate rage or fear? No.

Some people say women would never commit serial killings if they were not talked into it by male partners. That is a strong state- ment, and probably reckless. Still, it is a fact that one third of all fe- male serial killers have operated only as a member of a team,* never murdering except in the context of a killer partnership. Further, the women encountered within the following pages had little or no criminal history of any sort.

If research suggests that women who ultimately "terminated" other humans never displayed a violent temperament prior to hook- ing up with a killer, then we must delve further into these women's minds — and, hopefully, find clues to the explanations for such de- viant choices. What *does* allow a woman the capacity to murder? What is it about her loyalty or "love" for the serial killer that per- suades her to make his path her own? What are they lacking, that prevents others from falling prey to the manipulations of a conspira- tor? In such cases, men consumed with sexual fantasies, an obses- sion with "possessing" a woman entirely, turn their lovers into ac- complices who stay and cooperate, when other women might have fled.

*Michael Kelleher, *Murder Most Rare*.

*Male/Female Lust Killers*

This is not to rule out the woman's responsibility entirely. She may be a lust killer. Generally speaking, this is the largest group of serial killers. Sexual gratification is their primary motivation. And often, the female will work without provocation from her male part-ner, clearly exhibiting a sadistic tendency on her own. Contrary to what we may suppose (maniacal, clearly psychotic?) the female lust killer is among the most organized of team killers. She is not driven by fear or intimidation. She has not been "led" into a life of escalat-ing crime, gradually finding herself hostage to her partner and to the fear of being caught. She is completely unscrupulous and highly sys-tematic, generating levels of success that far exceed other female/male team killers. Her willingness and her excitement fuel a desire to control, to plan, and above all, to not be caught. Her only satisfac-tion comes from killing; so she is, within the subculture of murder, the most calculating and most successful.

Often, both members of a lust team begin their crime before the actual act, through fantasy — utilizing pornography in its vari-ous forms to gather ideas, to stimulate their drive. The killers create a very precise image of the victim, and the hunt begins. Like the fan-tasy, this period varies according to the killer. It may take weeks or months to find the right victim, and the predators may search sev-eral states. Finally comes the murder. For the lust killers, this is most personal. They often take home a souvenir body part, photos, tokens to stimulate later memories. And they use their hands as weapons, to make the act more personal and intimate. The post-death period may bring them a sense of emptiness, and a desire to confess, along with the realization that the only way to find satis-faction is to repeat the behavior.

Gradually, as in the homosexual teams, the weaker team mem-ber becomes increasingly insecure and resentful of her partner's re-lations with the victims. She transfers her repressed jealousy and her sense of betrayal to the victims, even as she engages in "shared" sexual relations. As her anger becomes harder to conceal, she becomes more vicious. Usually within the first year, her rage starts to erode the degree of organization that had guided the couples' activity; thus, most teams are caught in less than twelve months — although there are others who went on killing for many years.

As the female becomes less competent, her partner finds himself less fulfilled. Friction builds within the team. The couple becomes more vicious, opportunistic and even public — perhaps adding an armed robbery to a kidnapping. The crimes are egregious, and the use of weaponry escalates: knives, ropes, torture instruments are used; needless to say, the victims are often raped and brutalized, not simply killed. Once the victims are dead, the weapons are used to mutilate and dismember the bodies. It is not unusual for the male to gratify his need between events by masturbating while reliving a previous kill. He often will use a part of a victim's body — a head, a foot, some trophy appendage — to help achieve climax. The female partner takes on the bizarre role of caring for the token. Carol Bundy is the leading example in this category.

How are the men able to mold these women? What makes the women so vulnerable to their influence? A dedicated mother will abandon her children. A nurse will give up her work. Female team killers are stripped of their previous identities; their personalities go to pieces. They become simple accomplices in their men's sexual, murderous fantasies. But we must look deeper — why is this possible? By any account, this team killer has become monstrous in her deeds.

The innocuous monikers "Motherly Rose and Friendly Fred" shielded the couple that lived at 25 Cromwell Street in Gloucester, England from their real, more horrific identities. Indeed, Rosemary West and her common-law husband were perhaps the most infamous team killers in Britain's history. The couple seemed anything but infamous — unless you had personal experience with them.

Rosemary West had eight children; she was motherly, on the surface, and her husband was friendly. But underneath, these partners lived a life of pathology, sexual sadism and murder whose acts continued for two decades. That's a unique record; most team killers don't "last" for more than a year — two years is considered a kind of hallmark of longevity.

Rosemary Pauline Letts was born into a failing family on November 29, 1953, in Devon, England. She had six brothers and sisters, but it was she who received, as a young child, the sexual advances of her abusive father. He introduced Rosemary to incest; her passive mother abandoned her, leaving her with the brutal man while taking the other five children away. Apparently, she saw Rosemary as some sort of "lover" and threat. The child was thus left to her father's perversions.

The 27-year-old Frederick West came into her life in 1968. Frederick claimed he'd separated from his wife. Probably largely because of the personal issues she was struggling with (her experiences having set the stage for a fixation on "fatherly" figures with sexually dysfunctional desires), Rosemary took up with the bachelor, and accepted his sexual compulsions.

Frederick immediately lured her into a torrid and perverse affair. She was convinced that Frederick was a source of security — he found her appealing, and, as she was familiar with his "ways," she quickly moved in with him, playing the role of his lover and the nanny to his two daughters. She was fifteen.

Rosemary's father was intensely jealousy of her lover. He came and took her home, demanding that she never see Frederick again. This only drove Rosemary deeper into the young man's arms, and a rage that originated from early years of abuse created an even more determined obsession for Fred and her new life. She was intent on leaving her father behind. She went back to Fred's. Her father brought in the Social Services, and had her placed under British protective custody.

A year later, at the age of sixteen, she could no longer be held by the Crown. She and Frederick re-united, and she became, once again, a pseudo-nanny/mother to Anne Marie and Charmaine. In spite of her various roles, Rosemary's center was her sex. She was compelled to be with Frederick. She demonstrated her need to mate with this man by taking his last name prior to marriage. She was determined to forge a union, and she felt "righteous in her final act of defiance against [my] father," as she testified in her own trial, years later.

Fred and Rosemary, still not legally married, moved into their first home at 25 Midland Road in Gloucester, in October of 1970. They held wild parties, centered on sex and drugs, with the happy participation of their "enabling" friends and neighbors. Rosemary became pregnant that year, and Frederick felt sexually frustrated. His young lover helped him lure neighbors into their home for sex. Though they had already enjoyed free, open affairs with others, it excited Fred more to engage in unwarranted, unwanted sex.

Early on, a female neighbor was unwittingly drugged by the Wests. She later realized that she'd escaped the claws of death by a fraction. She found herself awakening in the early morning light, lying in a bed between the two Wests, and realized she'd been as-saulted. This was the beginning of the sexual path that would be-come an insatiable obsession for the Wests, as a couple: manipulat-ing and violating the unsuspecting. That was their ultimate high.

Rosemary's first child was born on October 17, 1979: Heather West. As a mother, her envy and jealousy toward Frederick's chil-dren, Anne Marie and Charmaine, created a frenzy. She tried to draw her husband's attention away from his first two daughters. She was horrifically abusive to both, particularly Charmaine. Friends would later recall the intimidating and abusive tactics Rosemary used to control the children. This lasted until May 22, 1971, when eight-year-old Charmaine vanished.

Meanwhile, Fred had been given a brief term in prison for theft. Rosemary was interrogated in regard to the sudden disap-pearance of the child, but she maintained that Charmaine had gone to live with her mother. The same year, shortly after Fred's release from prison, nine-year-old Anne Marie became the victim of incest and abuse: a predictable development in the West family. Anne Marie endured incest until she was fifteen and became pregnant with her father's child. She suffered a miscarriage, and left home.

Anne Marie would testify much later, at her mother's trial, that she believed her parents abused her for her own good. Brainwashed, she'd come to endure her pain as a sort of learning experience — discipline.

The Wests moved to the notorious 25 Cromwell Street in 1972. By now, drugs and sex were the centerpieces of the Wests' life. There were several rooms in the home, and some of them the couple rented to lodgers, mostly students and runaways. Behind the closed doors of this filthy, decrepit flat, far from the sight of witnesses, it was easy to turn their tenants into sex partners. To round out the numbers, they would entice people to come home with them after an evening at a pub — for a night of mayhem. Neither Rosemary nor Fred had a particular penchant for either gender; they had their fun, one way or another.

In 1973, Linda Gough, aged 20, left her home after an argument with her mother. Gough had already been to the Cromwell residence as a visitor; a male friend of hers had been a lodger. Not sure where she should go, she thought maybe this would do. Gough calmed herself, then notified her mother, after arriving at the lodgings. This would be the last conversation between mother and daughter. She was drugged, raped and murdered; her body was hidden and not discovered for many, many years.

In the years to follow, tenants came and went, moving in and out incessantly. Rosemary sold her body to prostitution with some of the tenants, and meanwhile she catered to her husband's insatiable need for voyeurism. She even helped design a "chamber" with a peephole, all arranged to accommodate the husband's pastime. Referred to as "Rosie's room," there was a collection of sex toys which they used on each other as well as on their willing — and unwilling — guests. Rosemary took to bondage, and developed a collection of tools to complement the many scenarios her bizarre mind would conjure up.

She was constantly pregnant in the next ten years, bearing

children from many different men. Her last child was born in 1983. Of course, Frederick bragged of fathering at least forty children — in a direct competition with his promiscuous wife. All, he claimed, were born to women victims at Cromwell.

But of all the children, "visitors," and wife, he had a growing fantasy for one victim: Heather. He seemed to be lurking, waiting for her to blossom into adolescence. To the ordinary observer, the Wests seemed normal, even loving. Rosemary appeared to take a normal interest in parenting. Neighbors saw them playing in the yard, where Frederick had built a swing set and planted a garden. But for those who knew, and had lived through the horrors of Cromwell, the Wests were the personification of evil.

Heather turned fourteen in 1985. Frederick's attentions toward her intensified, and he made her his primary sex partner. He was horrified and enraged when she resisted. He hadn't experienced such rejection from Anne Marie!

In 1987, Heather announced that she was leaving home. With a paranoid fear of what she might tell the police, Frederick strangled her. Then, using an ice saw, he removed her head and legs, and put all the pieces into a garbage bag with her torso. He buried the bag in a shallow grave in the garden.

"I can't believe we ate from that garden," a younger brother noted, years after his mother's arrest.

Frederick West would later claim that his wife was out shopping when the murder took place. And according to later testimony, Rosemary claimed that she had been told that her daughter had run off with her girlfriend, a lesbian. But evidence would prove that, in fact, Rosemary was present during her daughter's murder and dismemberment. Heather was sixteen.

This event did not engender any remorse, nor did it prohibit the abuse of other children. But in four years, this all would come to a stop: Frederick was charged with sexual abuse against his thirteen-year-old daughter (whose name remains undisclosed) in August 1991. Then, in an unexpected twist, because of the child's fear, she refused to testify against her father. The charges were formally dropped in 1992; but the investigator followed her instinct, determined to put Frederick West away and protect the child.

Detective Constable Hazel Savage of the Gloucester Police befriended the girl, while pursuing her investigation, and this proved pivotal to the investigation. The constable had many reasons to fear for the girl's life, as well as her siblings'; nevertheless, the girl shielded her parents inexorably. Constable Savage tried to get the child to tell her more about her older sister, Heather. In a sudden admission, she told the constable that, "If [she] said anything, her daddy said she'd end up in the garden next to her sister."

Savage was stunned. The investigation could now go forward on the basis of this preliminary evidence. She maintained her loving and nurturing stance while she continued her investigation — and this helped the other siblings to talk. She was able to convince Detective Superintendent John Bennett to obtain a search warrant. On February 24, 1994, an undercover detective walked into the backyard at Cromwell. The next day, the Wests were taken into custody on suspicion of murder.

Fred confessed, and told the investigators precisely where Heather's body could be located. On February 26, a skull was uncovered in a corner of the garden, and the rest of the remains were also found. Heather was identified by dental records; clearly, she had not gone off on a lark with her friend.

In the next few days, eight bodies were discovered in the yard, including Gough's, which had been missing since 1973. Shirley Robertson, eighteen years old and a former resident and participant (eight months pregnant when she'd disappeared) was found not far from Heather's burial The aborted fetus was buried nearby. Allison Chambers, last heard from in September 1977 when she wrote to her

mother on her seventeenth birthday, was found under the patio, naked and bound, with a belt fastened around her skull. Near her body
were the remains of Lucy Partington, niece of author Kingsley Amis,
aged twenty-one. Her jaw still wore a tattered gag. The findings
included five other bodies in the basement: Therese Siegenthaler, 21,
a Swiss national who had disappeared while hitchhiking in 1984;
Juanita Mott, eighteen, who had disappeared April 1974; Shirley
Hubbard, fifteen; and Carol Cooper, eighteen, who had vanished
while walking home after spending the afternoon with her elderly
grandmother. Body number five has never been identified.

Frederick West received nine counts of murder, but adamantly
insisted that he'd worked alone. "He was frightened that there'd be
no one to look after us; I really think that's what he was considering," says one of his daughter, now a mother living outside of
Gloucester. Rosemary was sent home, as there was no evidence on
which to convict her.

Fred admitted to his oldest son Steven that he'd killed before — he murdered Anne McFall, a lover, in 1967. He described
where he'd hidden her body. She was pregnant at the time. He followed that by murdering his wife, Rena, in 1969, on New Year's Day.
He said the bodies would be found in a rural area near his boyhood
home in Much Marcle, Herefordshire.

Only Rena and Anne were found. After these discoveries, the
authorities were certain that Charmaine had met with a similar demise; they found her, in a state of decomposition, under the kitchen
floor at 25 Midland.

Rosemary was charged with Heather's and Charmaine's
deaths — ten counts, altogether. It was the end of 1994, and Mrs.
West's prospects were grim. How could she evade the police? It
looked as though this dangerous woman finally would be imprisoned. But then Mr. West came to her rescue: Frederick backed her
up, and the case was circumstantial at best: no witnesses, no finger

prints. . . nothing. The prosecution's hands were tied. Then Brian Leveson, Queen's Counsel, had a brainstorm — the break he needed. With Justice Mantell presiding as judge, the prosecutor was allowed to act on his idea; he brought in the testimony of three survivors of sexual attacks from both Frederick and Rosemary West. On the grounds of "similar fact evidence," the West case turned in favor of the Crown, as it became clear that Rosemary was capable of extreme sexual pathology.

Frederick's attempts to protect Rosemary were in vain. She would have to face trial. Confronted with that unbearable prospect, he committed suicide in his prison cell, on New Year's Day, 1995, leaving the "wife" he'd tried to spare utterly alone to face up to their mutual atrocities.

The Crown Prosecution Service concluded that it was highly unlikely that Rosemary West was ignorant of her "husband's" actions. Nine of the victims found had been dismembered; all the victims had been sexually abused. Masterminding and managing so much mayhem would have entailed an enormous amount of work. How could he have hidden it from another adult who shared the flat? He couldn't.

Leveson pleaded with the jury to think of the evidence against Rosemary West as "three brass monkeys: she saw nothing, heard nothing, and said nothing." This darkly humorous argument was convincing, and with that the jury went off to deliberate in a hotel room, on November 20, 1995, after 28 days of testimony. Finally, Rosemary received justice: ten counts of murder, ten counts of life imprisonment.

Rosemary has been given the right to respond to her mail. A cryptic note in response to my questions is in keeping with her husband's attempts to maintain her innocence.

*I am not much for interviews. I realize my husband was ill, but he says himself the truth, so I need not repeat that. I will forever serve punishment for his crime. I will always love him, however; it was indeed sickness that drove him. It was very much a possibility to share our room, and not share in each other's lives completely. Records and witnesses can discount these efforts to hang me....*

*Rosemary*

## CATHERINE AND DAVID BIRNIE

While this team did not go on killing for the one- to two-year period that many manage, it might well have surpassed the standard "spree" if not for the miraculous escape of the couple's last victim.

In the early 1970s, David Birnie met his future wife, Catherine Johnston. Alone, neither Australian-born individual appeared capable of mustering even a hint of violence. David Birnie was diminutive, with awkward features and thick glasses. Catherine was nondescript at best. She was often passed over for dates, and was noted as being "quiet to a fault" by family members.

Catherine met David when they were both in their teens. But David had already spent time in mental institutions, having been diagnosed with learning disabilities. In between hospitalizations, the two shared the same high school. Finally, here was a man who showed interest in Catherine; and he was elated to find a woman who reciprocated his affection — which rapidly grew into a heated sexual appetite. Catherine was happy to oblige. Together with

David's growing sexual confidence, he evolved a sense of self and a generalized sense of power.

David and Catherine began discussing more than their future love life together; they pondered how they could support themselves at a much higher level than their families had achieved. Through robbery, they could spend a minimum of time working — and, most important, they could spend all their time together. Catherine, insecure and unwilling to separate from her lover, was willing to acquiesce to David's scheme.

But life as small-time crooks didn't pan out too well: they were caught after their third theft, a gas station robbery in a small Australian community called Willagee.

Apprehended, David and Catherine were sent to separate juvenile detention centers. Upon release, each married someone else — though a torch still burned. Between 1979 and 1985, Catherine had five children with her husband, a man she'd met while working at a menial job in a mill. But Catherine could not forget her first love, and soon after the birth of her fifth and last child, she decided to confront David, who also still lived near Willagee. She confessed her undying love. The feelings were mutual, and both of them left spouses — and children — for this re-ignited passion. They divorced their spouses and married each other in early 1985.

Apparently, David's sex drive had escalated over the years. Within eighteen months, he was introducing his bride to themes much darker than compulsive sex or a desire to steal; he divulged his fantasy to possess a sex slave.

Catherine was despondent to hear that her husband needed another lover, but she was more agitated by the idea of being separated from him again. She agreed to participate in his fantasy to find a woman for use as a sex toy. The relationship he contemplated seemed one-dimensional; Catherine's envy was appeased by the thought that David couldn't "love" another, he only meant to fulfill a sexual urge.

Between October 6 and November 10, 1986, David would be allowed to fulfill his "urge" four times.

The Birnies ran an ad offering used tires for sale. Mary Neilson, 22, responded, and agreed to meet the couple at their home. The attack was disorganized: David had not clearly planned when he would make his move. He had not been sure the visitor would suit his needs — until he laid eyes on the pretty young student. He found himself aroused. At knifepoint, David ordered the woman to undress, and he raped her. Part of his fantasy was that Catherine should watch. When David announced that he was "finished," he and his wife drove their victim to the Glen Eagle National Park, where David once again violated the young woman; then he mutilated her with his knife, and finally strangled her to death. Her body was hastily buried in a shallow grave.

It had been so easy and exhilarating. David now actively sought another victim. Catherine was slightly surprised when her husband brought what seemed to be a mere child to their home at Moorhouse Road — a 15-year-old hitchhiker. After several days, it seemed that Birnie was starting to develop a relationship with his victim: something that ignited enormous rage in Catherine. That had not been part of his original "pitch." David seemed to be thinking of allowing the hostage an indefinite stay. Catherine took it upon herself to strangle the young girl, ridding herself of this threat.

The third victim died less painfully. Noelene Patterson, in her early twenties, was acquainted with the killers. She readily accepted a ride when the Birnies offered to pick her up after her car broke down. After three days of sexual exploits and humiliation, the Birnies provided Noelene with sleeping pills so that she would not endure the pain of her inevitable strangulation.

Denise Brown was abducted on November 4, 1986. She was held captive for two days before David grew bored. He stabbed her to death and dumped her body in the pines of Wanneroo.

On November 7, the Birnies kidnapped a fifth victim. Like her predecessors, Thelma Cree, 20, was held at their home. David seemed to take an enormous liking to her; meanwhile, Catherine had grown accustomed to her husband's pattern, feeling less jealous and more accepting of each sex victim/partner. Both had let their guard down: Catherine, assuming that David was in control of his victim, and David, in a semi-delusional state, believing that his victim had grown accustomed to her environment and was not necessarily desperate to escape.

And so David went out for an evening walk, while Catherine dozed, off and on. Young Thelma took advantage of the moment and escaped through a back door. Half-naked, she made her way to a neighboring community, Fremantle, and crept into a little grocery market. In shock and in tears, she told the workers there of the nightmare she'd been through; they called the authorities.

David and Catherine were under arrest within two hours of her escape. Neither pointed a finger, nor put up a fight. They made no attempt to deny the charges.

Within six months, both had been given life sentences, and Catherine had led the police to all the bodies. David and Catherine made full confessions to four rapes and four murders.

The March 3, 1987 trial lasted less than thirty minutes. Judge Waller cited "remarkable violence, and grave cause to look at the power resultant when virtually harmless people join to forge a lethal union — that needs further scrutiny."

Judge Waller's statement held a universal truth; like many cases examined in these pages, a certain level of sexual deviancy may have existed in both individuals, but the boldness to act out only materialized with the support of the "unit." His remark leaves the reader to question how many people might have avoided a ghastly fate, if not for the horrifying marriage of two volatile minds?

DEBRA DENISE BROWN AND ALTON COLEMAN

During my research for another project, I came across the story of Alton Coleman. Psychologists described him as intermittently "charming and charismatic, then threatening and deadly." I found out for myself — this was more than true. My own experience with this serial killer helped me gain insight into the forms of manipulation, the tactics used to lure, to threaten, to persuade and to finally entrap a woman — even a journalist who already knew enough to be terrified by the man behind the bars. Perhaps, by studying how these men operate, conning even the more "seasoned" of us with their deceit, we may achieve greater insight into just how the dynamic might work when they forge intimate relationships with women.

I kept journal entries as I communicated with serial killers, studying what ignites their rage, and their desire to possess and to "terminate." In April, 1977, I wrote about Alton Coleman.

*God, it was such a beautiful day... I can't recall the last time we did-n't have at least some rain in a day. I actually wore shorts and a halter top, hoping the sun would roast my pasty skin. Everything was going so well; we needed a family day. And then I got a call from Alton Coleman. I'm incredibly confused. I can't believe I allowed him to get my phone number. He wrote in his letters that he would like to talk more in-depth about his crimes, but considering that all his letters are read [before being released, by the prison staff] and the phones are only randomly recorded, he needed to talk by phone. NEVER had I received a letter from him that frightened me; I thought he was genuinely remorseful; not actually "rehabilitated" or anything crazy like that — but his de-meanor allowed me to believe that, compared to his past, his way of dealing with women, and compared to most of the men I'm dealing with, he was at least willing to look at what he'd done. Here's a letter:*

*Dear Jenny,*

*I have remorse and things I wish to say but only by phone. I can't bear the thought of my letters being read by strangers in mail rooms... call you Saturday, Feb 13 at noon up. Please be there... you know I did it — from seven to seventy years — I did it... praise you for helping me... at least, wanting to...*

*A. Coleman*

I feel humiliated, unprofessional. As it turns, he had some sort of plan to scare the heck out of me — it worked. But that it was all *planned*, that was scarier than what he said; this... Jekyll and Hyde. I can't shake it. It's as if, had I been in the room with him, I would have been too terrified not to obey; I don't know... I was just taken off guard, which is exactly what he intended. There we were: my husband watering the roses, splashing the kids with the hose, I was mowing the lawn and the kids had propped their plastic slide against the wading pool. We were having a great day. Then the phone rang. Dean picked it up — I'd told him I was expecting a call from the penitentiary, "Georgia Pen" — so he accepted charges and handed me the phone. I ran for the porch and away from the splashing, hoping I'd be able to hear over the ruckus — I wish I hadn't. I was nervous, my hands twitched; I accidentally hit "record" on my phone; probably the smartest thing I did today. . . it says it all. So I think I'll just play it back. Here we go. . .

"Collect from Georgia State. Alton Coleman."

"Alton — you got my number. I know the routine — a few minutes. So shoot. What was so intense you couldn't say it in a letter?"

"So how's you feels about us niggers? You like the feel of us on you, bitch?"

"What? What are you saying?"

"Those other gals, the ones you's tellin' me you got to know about cuz you's got it up you ass you some kind a help to change the world, is shit. You's makin money and I'll tell you how I cut the throat of a baby girl from side to side if it means I be getting a cut off the top — A *big* fuckin cut or you be getting fuckin cut, got that, writer-bitch?"

"Don't call me again."

"But you be given me your number. I got your permission, girl — wha? You be scarin yourself? Maybe shoulda thought on that before you's get yourself all's in atangle, out here with us boys. Pretty thing — I'd fuck you too. . . saw you's on TV about this book. Now don't you be lyin anymore about this is some study — you's on TV, you's gettin rich. I ain' sayin another thing til I gets me my money."

"Don't. I don't want to talk to you again. I'll have my phone blocked."

"But I's been doin this game a lot longer, bitch. I don't need to cut you — you cut your own nose to spite yourself — you cut me off, you cut off. Get it? No calls from any your boys. No book, no money. Got to keep me on the inside. Wish I could be inside you —

Damn! Whew you be hot! We all says that bout you in here. . . "

I slammed the receiver down.
Seconds later it rang.

"H-hello?"
"Collect from Georgia — please, bitch, I's only — you take this — I means I sorry. . ."
How could he get past the operators? I didn't understand. I didn't understand anything.
"Fuck me!"
That sounds terrible, but after that exchange. . . that about summed it up.

All I could do was sit back in my red chair and hug myself. The sun hit my body through the window but I was still shaking. I kept telling myself: Get it together. For them, please God, let me pull it together. . . I could hear the kids laughing outside — Dean was protesting about a dog pile, or so it appeared through the window.

I walked back out and sat on the porch. It still smelled of fresh paint. I took a deep breath. I grabbed some Cokes from the fridge. Pop is usually a big no-no, but not right then. Anything to lift the day. . . and I didn't want them to know, to see how frightened I was.

Dennis and Frances squealed like two urchins being fed bread after weeks of starvation. I told them to slow down (God, what is it about Coke?) and I threw one to Dean. He grabbed just in time and smiled. He didn't know, and I couldn't decide whether to tell him — it seemed. . . weak. I remember I said:

"Well, big, strong mommy is going back to the mean, scary mower and that awful, gargantuan lawn on our steep, steep hill to make everything look pretty. Wish me luck!" It was like I was doing overkill on happy-mommy talk to compensate for this monster I'd inadvertently allowed into our world.

As I mowed, I noticed my body wasn't strong. Like my mind, my body was moving slowly — I felt stunned, in some way. I tried to move the mower up the hill, but found it was pushing my trembling legs backward. He made me have to stop. What a psychological invasion. Imagine, Debra. . . I wanted to talk with her. I felt so fragile, I literally had to call to Dean to grab the mower. I was on my knees. I went from fear to nausea. I threw up, right there in our front yard. I turned away from the kids, I hoped they couldn't see. Dean knew. He rubbed my back and told me he could feel my bones. Great — just what I felt like hearing. He said he was worried and why didn't I eat like a horse anymore?

I couldn't tell him. It's so weird, because I think it's about fearing what he'd say: stop the book. And I really just can't. So I'm writing it down, instead. My stomach feels strange. I feel like a captive; I need to shake it, it's what these guys want. It's the disease of it all. I'm not much good to anyone if I stay in "victim-mode." And that's not who I am.

Victim mode. What puts the killer accomplice in a dual role of victim and perpetrator? Each case is unique, but all share commonalities — suggestibility, dysfunctional or transient home life, a desire to "connect" deeply, to be needed, to feel sexually desirable. . . the woman's intelligence level is not usually more than median; her job is rarely more than menial. The man brings to this women's world a sense of excitement, romance and thrill. And then it is thrust upon her: his secret desire to kill.

So, does she give up the person with whom she has a cherished intimate relationship? Has she done something to create this desire in him — is it her fault? He says it's just for fun, or it's a show of loyalty, and it rarely begins with murder. Pornography, bondage, then assault, a robbery — a walk on the "wild side." It's not so unbearable.

And then the killing begins. The result is a sense of "we're alone in the world, this is our secret," which ignites a special sense of belonging. Or, "Oh, God. . . what have I done? What will he do to me?" — a sense of entrapment. The women rarely will tell you themselves which way they feel. They are either protecting, or living in fear. So the information is here, but the judgment is left to the reader.

Debra Denise Brown (no relation to the victim in the previous chapter) was born in 1963 into a family of eleven children. She only knew poverty. Unlike the psychological diagnosis that called Coleman both charming and deadly, Debra has been described by prison counselors as "exceedingly passive and easily manipulated."

When she met Alton in 1984, she decided to break off her engagement to another man. She was only 21, but her life had been fairly dismal and though she was not exceedingly bright, circumstances had given her a somewhat worldly outlook. She had lived in extreme poverty, dropping out of high school and working menial jobs to help her family. Alton seemed like an answer to her prayers: he was funny, and always seemed to have enough money for a good time; in a matter of weeks, she moved in with him. They took up residence in her hometown, Waukegan, Illinois.

She had no idea that Alton had come to town on the lam, jumping bail after charges were brought against him for the rape of a fourteen-year-old. Debra would have to learn for herself Alton's propensity for wild, even vicious sex. As soon as they moved in together, he displayed his "desires," with Debra becoming the focus of his unbridled sexual deviance and physical violence.

Her life of poverty had taught her hunger; life with Alton was an awakening to all things evil — and yet, he was always "sorry." And he possessed charm; when he wasn't after her sexually, or succumbing to attacks of rage, he was charismatic. Denise told herself that Alton, who'd already explained he'd come from a broken home, would get over his anger if she continued to love him. Alton left out all the pieces of his past that might have made her think otherwise, that perhaps she wasn't "special" enough to overcome Alton's troubled psyche.

Born in 1956, Alton lived with his mother, a prostitute, until her death. He was barely a teenager. He had witnessed her sexual activities, and had been asked to solicit to some of her clients who had a taste for boys. Alton repressed his rage, but never seemed to recover from the sexual abuse he encountered. His history reflects that of an incredibly angry, disoriented boy. By twelve, he was considered a "career" criminal. He'd robbed, assaulted, stolen cars and been charged for possession of a deadly weapon. His grandmother took him in, hoping that without his mother's influence, he might "recover." Unfortunately, the damage was done, ingrained. His nickname was "Pissy," because he wet his pants frequently at school. That increased his rage as well as his need to vindicate himself, somehow.

He could not escape the behavioral and psychological manifestations of childhood abuse. By the time he met up with Debra, he'd served hard time: three years in a state prison for three counts — robbery, assault and sexual molestation. His sexual rage became evident in prison, where he earned a reputation as a violent sexual offender — for Alton, sex was only about power, and venting. Of course, this part of Alton's history was hidden from Debra.

Authorities still question the extent of Debra's participation in the mayhem and murder that took place over a two-month period, across six states. One family member explained,

> *One day, she's about to marry this pretty-okay guy, and the next, Alton shows up out of thin air. I didn't know what to think, it all happened so fast. She was a good sister, a good person. Just really, really*

*quiet. So I wonder all the time if she knows what happened, either. Just took off with him, and maybe she was scared, but I know, by the time they was caught, they think she'd killed two people herself. That ain't my sister.*

*— Anonymous*

It was that quick. Debra has only allowed that it was fast:

*(I) couldn't be the target of his violence. When we took off, I just didn't get it. But that's all I want to say about any of it.*

*Debra Denise Brown*

And so she helped him find other targets. Experts agree that Alton was clearly the dominant person — choosing victims and planning their road trips, what places to rob — no explanations. Debra's job was to play poor — beg for money. She knew that role.

The couple took on aliases, as Paul and Diana Fisher. Together they barged into an acquaintance's house and took off with nine-year-old Vernita Wheat; Alton beat her, raped her, then strangled her to death. Within three weeks, Alton found an even more appealing scenario: two little girls. They were now seventy miles south, in Gary, Indiana. On June 18, 1984 they managed to murder seven-year-old Tamika Turks, but although they stabbed her nine-year-old cousin, the child miraculously survived. "It was too easy. We just said we'd give 'em a ride. That was all," Coleman explained to me. Tamika's companion was able to describe the couple vividly, but Debra and Alton had fled to Toledo, Ohio, where they knocked on the door of Virginia Temple and her daughter, Rochelle, aged ten; they pretended to be penniless hitchhikers who needed a place to stay the night. The mother and daughter were assaulted, then strangled. And Debra and Alton moved on.

On July 11, they were in Detroit. Donna Williams was found strangled, her body hidden in a tenement building. She had been kidnapped from Gary by a couple, and witnesses described them pretty well. Still, Debra and Alton continued their rampage. In Cincinnati, Marlene Waters and her husband were attacked in their home. It was July 13. Tragically, Mrs. Waters died from her injuries; but her husband survived and again, a description was provided to authorities.

Coleman was incredibly "disorganized." In criminal justice terms, that means that he quickly became sloppy in his approach to the crimes. Killers fall into three sub-categories: lust, power-seekers, and thrill-killers. Alton Coleman crossed all lines: he killed, sometimes as a follow-up to sexual violating the victim (lust); he killed to satiate his sense of grandiosity — to fulfill his sense of dominance or power over his victim; and he killed, sometimes, simply because (as he has said), "[I] enjoy myself when I'm killing. . . ." While lust killers are the most calculated amongst the categories, both power killers and thrill killers tend to escalate in their killing mode, allotting less time to planning. They have less fun in the planning phase, although that phase is important to the lust killer's pleasure (finding the appropriate victim, following her/him — sometimes for months — and fantasizing, which may include the use of pornographic material and acting out the "future" crime in a play-like version). Alton vented his rage by committing several murders in a very short span of time. He became less methodical, less controlled.

When the serial killer stops planning, he becomes easier prey for investigators. He leaves evidence behind: blood, semen, weapons, a license plate. Indeed, when Alton was finally captured, he was carrying bloodied knives in his pockets. Mindlessly, the couple made their escape from the Waters' house in Marlene Water's car (although, with police hot on their trail, Alton did think to ditch the car fairly quickly). He landed himself on the Federal Bureau of Investigation's "Most Wanted" list in July, 1984, less than two months after the spree had begun.

He was nowhere near ending his binge of victimizing and murdering. He and Debra made it to Indianapolis, where they lured in 15-year-old Tonnie Stewart with a sad tale of hunger pains and no money. Alton grabbed her, forced her into their latest stolen vehicle and proceeded to assault, then strangle her. Tonnie's body was found in a vacant building in an urban area of Indianapolis, an impoverished neighborhood known for drugs, prostitution and violence The couple then broke into the home of Ms. Eugene Scott, aged 77, and shot her to death. Her body was found in a ditch just outside Indianapolis.

In their spare time, Debra and Alton plundered their way through city and state, robbing and assaulting, leaving behind live witnesses on almost every block — all describing the same two persons. The work of authorities and civilians together led to their apprehension in Evanston, Illinois. A man recognized Coleman from the "Wanted" program on television, and called in. The police were contacted and went to work, combing the city until the couple was found. At the time of his arrest, Alton Coleman was carrying two knives stained with blood and Debra Brown was packing a .38 caliber pistol.

The next chapter in this horrific story was an argument between the states: who would get to take the first shot at a trial. Ultimately, the couple was tried in a variety of counties, and Ohio was chosen as their new "home." Bail was set a $25 million for Alton and $20 million for Debra, until all the trials should be completed.

In Illinois, Alton was convicted in January 1987 of the aggravated kidnapping and murder of Vernita Wheat, and sentenced to die by lethal injection.

In Cincinnati, Ohio, in May of 1985, the two were tried separately for the murder of Marlene Waters. Alton was sentenced to die in the electric chair while Debra Brown was given life imprisonment. In August of 1985, the killers were transferred to Dayton, Ohio. Both received 20-year sentences for kidnapping. Once again in separate trials, in April of 1986, the couple faced murder charges in the case of Tamika Turks in Indiana. The courts attached the rape and attempted murder of her cousin. Coleman was again sentenced to death plus 100 years' imprisonment. His charge: attempted murder and rape. Debra Brown was also given the death sentence plus two consecutive 40-year terms. Then, on June 8, they were tried separately for the murder of Tonnie Stewart, and both were sentenced to death. Governor Richard Celest of Ohio commuted one of Brown's death sentences to life imprisonment in 1991, as he retired.

Debra will be most remembered for a statement made during one of her trials: "I had fun out of it." A counselor retorts, "What else was she going to say? Alton was staring at her from across the room." The jury is still out, on that.

Today, they both appeal their convictions from separate prisons in Ohio.

## CYNTHIA COFFMAN AND JAMES GREGORY MARLOW

In a rampage that crisscrossed Arizona and California, James Gregory Marlow murdered four persons with the aid of Cynthia Coffman. During their five-week spree in 1986, the killing was foreshadowed by robberies and sexual assaults.

Cynthia was an active participant in all the murders, which resulted in both a death sentence — and a life sentence. Some cases are difficult to understand. We can attempt to see the victimization of a woman and even her place as the "lured"; however, while experts agree that that description seems to hold for the majority of male/female team-killer relationships, it does not fit the profile of Cynthia Coffman.

Born in 1962, Cynthia Coffman was the daughter of a well-to-do and well-respected family from St. Louis, Missouri. Her home environment provided both a deeply religious tone and a respectable and stable home life, very "Leave it to Beaver," as she herself has described her childhood.

But at seventeen, Cynthia became pregnant by her teenage sweetheart. She was forced into a marriage, which was racked by turmoil. She did attempt to make a go of it for five years. She finally left her husband, her home and her family, feeling disgraced and hoping she'd rebound with a new life. . . which she went off to seek in Arizona.

Cynthia landed a job as a waitress at a small café in the spring of 1985. She met a man. And within a few months, they were living together. This relationship was punctuated with chaos, drunkenness and drug addiction. By the end of 1985, things had gone to pieces. Evicted from their home because of their wild parties and other disturbances, the couple became drifters. Within a year, the lovers were slapped with felony charges for drugs possession.

Somehow, all the charges against Cynthia Coffman were dismissed, while her lover was sent to the county jail. In the midst of this dysfunctional relationship, during a visit to the jail, she met a heinous creature who would bring more chaos, more nightmares to her life than anyone who had known her could ever have dreamed. A teenage bride and mother-turned-drug-addict — Cynthia's life was dramatic enough already. Not even her closest friends thought her capable of becoming a murderess.

James Marlow was her lover's cellmate, and naturally Cynthia met him while visiting her boyfriend. She felt an immediate surge of electricity. Marlow was five years Cynthia's senior; he had a lifelong criminal history that included robbery, assault and theft. He was also a white supremacist — and Cynthia took to his "superior" belief system and intense dominance. In spite of his unpromising background, Cynthia was forthright about her feelings. She rejected her erstwhile lover for Marlow, and took up with him upon his release from prison.

They drove throughout the South, aimlessly. They borrowed money from relatives (his), and supplemented their finances by committing minor thefts. They both were unwilling to take jobs — they found crime more intriguing, an exciting means to make money. Their petty assaults and thefts escalated to felonious crimes. On July 26, 1986, while in Kentucky, James and Cynthia broke into a house, taking all the cash, weapons, jewelry and other valuables they could grab. Later in the week, giddy with love and excitement, they fled to Tennessee and were married. Cynthia had "I belong to the Folsom Wolf" tattooed across her buttocks. He took deep pride in this signature; this had been his moniker while imprisoned in California.

The couple felt untouchable, empowered by the robbery in Kentucky. They headed back west to familiar territory and that was when, on October 11, 1986, the couple committed their first known murder. They attacked a 32-year-old woman as she took cash from an ATM in Costa Mesa, California. They beat her, robbed her of her money, and then strangled the semiconscious woman to death. The body was carted to Riverside County, where it was discovered several weeks later.

Back in Arizona, they did it again. They were less impulsive, more methodical this time. Again at an ATM, they attacked a 35-year-old woman on October 28, 1986, and treated her the same as the first victim: beating, robbery, strangulation. They felt invincible.

On November 7, back in Redlands, California, they struck again, kidnapping a 20-year-old woman who had just used her ATM in a shopping center. Five days later, the couple would murder for the last (known) time: a 19-year-old student. Both of these last victims were also raped.

The escalation would have continued, according to psychologist Judy Mahoney of Seattle, Washington. But, as Dr. Mahoney explains, "Marlow and Coffman were careless in the aftermath of their crimes, while basking in their sense of glory. They had accomplished a workable method of operation, but they were haphazard, leaving evidence in their wake." Indeed, it was fairly easy to link the homicides to the perpetrators. A checkbook discarded by the killers was found, in a sack, together with papers that revealed their full names. Now that their identities were known, the media circulated their story.

Near Big Bear, California, authorities apprehended the couple, who had registered under their real names at a local motel. In some cases, the female partner turns on the male at the time they are caught. Unusually, Cynthia did not turn on James — at least, not initially. She confessed to her part in the murders, leading authorities to crime scenes and a missing victim. Nearly three years passed before a trial was announced, during which period James made accusations that forced Cynthia into an adversarial position.

In San Bernardino, California, on trial in July 1989, each was charged with a single count of murder. It was a hands-down case for the prosecution. The two were found guilty almost instantly. The next year, both were sentenced to death. Cynthia's death sentence holds a place in history: after the re-instatement of the death penalty in California in 1977, she was the first to be so sentenced. On May 14, 1992, Cynthia went back on trial in Orange County. The verdict: guilty. On September 26, 1992, the presiding judge sentenced her to life imprisonment.

Marlow awaits his death, pending the results of an appeal. In a previous letter, he wrote,

> *Dear Jenny,*
>
> *I know people think we done bad things. Me and her loved one another, but I never thought we would be in this mess. My woman, I did love her, but she got so jelus over things, including just robbing ladys. But she liked to do the same as me. There was more to her than anybody knows but me. She got thrown out because she hurt her folks the way she got pregnant and they wont get over it. She got angered about that and run off. I bet she could be lots of things if not for the way they act when*

she got pregnant. But I loved her, and there was parts to her that were not going to work out there in her life with her folks anyways. She got a thing for being crazy. She jump these women. I aint going to talk about that because I got my appeals, but she did have something to do with everything. One doctor here says with us, or anybody who does things like we did, in a pair, that we are both the same. She would like to think she could be different but she can only be who she is. I am sorry she would not talk to you. She is freaked that people will confuse her life story, take advantage. I want to talk and maybe then I can have my life, even if I can only have it here. I'm the WOLF. I can take care of myself. Wolf can survive anyplace and that's me. I was a WOLF there, just surviving any how I could. I did things out of order and people will judge me for that. Someday if I do die, I hope someone looks at my life, and can forgive me. For now I can say that when you know how it is to be a street person, and then the drugs, well, you don't think the same as some one like may be how you think. Like you got education and may be fam-ily and things. Then some one like me comes along and you and I meet on the street, and you are my target. My lunch. I do not mean that bad, its just that the street person and the other kind are different kinds, and I do what I do, I keep my belly full same as you. I'm just sorry some times and then I let my beast side get in the way, the sex of the WOLF. You might think its crazy talk. But just live my life, its not crazy. Just like to you the things you do aint crazy. You go to a store and by food. I don't know nothing about banks and checks and nothing like that. But I aint stupid. I find my own ways. My "Sin," that is what I call Cynthia, is a lot more like me than probly you but she just had different chances than me. Some things are just the way you are born. If you want more, than you can write to me. I do think some times on what it would be like if I hadn't loved her. I was going to get out. I would not be perfect but I would not be facing death nether.

L.W.

## CARIL ANN FUGATE AND CHARLES STARKWEATHER

A pattern can be detected in most team-killer cases. After reviewing many cases, the profile of the male, dominant figure becomes fairly predictable and the reader or researcher develops a sense that mitigating factors play an important role. They contribute to the male's rage, and his need (more often than not) to sexually possess and then destroy women; his background also helps explain how he uses his manipulative skills to draw his accomplice into his world, making her a very necessary component to his own success.

If any case demonstrates a female's sudden introduction into sadism, it is that of Caril Ann Fugate. She became involved with a killer nearly fifty years ago (in 1958); experts still refer to her case to illustrate just how persuasive the male perpetrator can be, and just how frightened his co-conspirator may be, no matter what her level of involvement. Caril Ann Fugate is often referred to as a "hostage" rather than a perpetrator, in spite of the appalling crimes she was privy to.

Caril Ann was born in Nebraska in 1944. Typically, she had no history of violence — until she hooked up with Charles Stark-weather. She was only fourteen. She did fairly well in school, hold-ing an average grade point; likewise, her social activities were nor-mal. She had her share of friends, some of whom still recall her has "a giddy child. . . happy." But some component of Caril Ann's per-sonality was searching for something more thrilling than her school-mates could provide. Charles would satisfy any need, filling that "void" beyond her wildest dreams — or nightmares. In interviews, she has claimed that although he was small (barely five foot two inches tall), "He was the most handsome creature (I'd) ever laid eyes on. He was volatile at times, he carried a rifle. I was aware of these things, but with me, he was very different. There was very little rage directed toward me; at most, [he was] perhaps moody."

But Starkweather was filled with rage. In Caril Ann he saw a perfect mate: she did not judge him or question him. Considering his past, that was crucial. He had plenty to hide, but Caril Ann seemed disinterested in anything about Charles that happened be-fore they met. Charles could be a "different person with Caril Ann," as he once stated. The young girl's parents were less impressed, and far less blinded by Starkweather' charms. And when they demanded that she discontinue seeing the young man, predictably, she was more attracted than ever. When Starkweather proposed they run off together, Fugate saw no alternative — a life solely without him, or solely with him. If only she had sharper instincts — but she was only a child.

Starkweather, 17 years old when he met Fugate, was decades older in life experience. From the time he could prattle his first words, Charles demonstrated an angry nature and aggressive behav-iors. As a small boy, his father ridiculed him for his "girlish ways." Eventually, Charles would spend all of his time away from home (which could only have been a relief to his family, considering the friction his presence appeared to cause).

Going it on his own was not so easy, either; he got plenty of ribbing in the real world as well. Charles also suffered physical disabilities, myopia and severely bowed legs. He felt very much alone. It was no surprise that Caril Ann's unquestioning, unconditional admiration would prove emotionally satisfying. Still, the endless taunting of peers, employers and family had done its damage: Charles had a bone to pick . . . with everyone. He dropped out of high school and supported himself by collecting garbage. He made it clear to his co-workers that he packed a gun and kept a rifle at close hand. His impulsive rage was becoming more apparent, and he picked fights at work on the least provocation. Other employees found working with him more than unbearable, they found Charles frightening. Even customers, when he picked up their garbage, avoided him. Some locked their doors. He found this amusing. Sometimes he'd get his rifle out, pretending to "shoot" at someone he felt was already fearful of him.

As he and Caril Ann discussed running off together, Charles began taking his job less and less seriously. His life in the farmland of Lincoln, Nebraska held nothing for him. Caril Ann waited docilely for Charles to pick that perfect moment to "saddle-up" and make his getaway, swinging her up on behind him as they rode off into the sunset.

On December 1, 1957 Charles Starkweather drove up to a small gas station, a neighborhood stop with a small market adjacent to the pumps, to carry out the first episode in what would become one of American's most famous crime sprees. His primary intention was a robbery. Tragically, he decided to abduct Robert Colvert, the 21-year-old attendant, at gunpoint. He forced Robert to drive, and headed for the outskirts of town. In an isolated area, far from any witnesses, Charles executed Robert with one shot in the back of the head. His body was discovered a few days later, but police found very little evidence at the crime scene — nothing left behind to identify a possible suspect. Meanwhile, an unsuspecting Caril Ann found the prospect of running off with her boyfriend more romantic with every passing day. She had no idea he had murdered Robert Colvert.

The time was finally right for the couple's planned departure. In fact, Charles had no choice but to flee. On January 21, 1958 the rebel pulled in front of Caril Ann's house and waited for her to arrive home from school. Her mother, Belda Bartlett, confronted him about his relationship with her daughter, demanding that he leave Caril Ann alone. She kept her point simple, saying only that Caril Ann was still a child — not daring to mention that Charles was too volatile, lest she ignite that very temper.

According to later testimony from Starkweather, he felt "paranoid" that Mrs. Bartlett found him inferior, and felt she was "talking down" to him. During the trial, he explained that he was smart enough to know that she was lying: that she was as fearful as worried about the relationship. And it made him angry — Starkweather found her fear a weakness, a justification for killing her. At the first sign of rejection, Starkweather lashed out physically at Mrs. Bartlett. A struggle ensued, and Starkweather shot her with his rifle, killing her. When her husband heard the gunshot, he ran to the scene, and Starkweather shot him to death, too.

Caril Ann arrived to find her parents' bloody bodies on the floor. Besides herself and her boyfriend, there was only one living "witness": two-year-old Betty Bartlett. In a frenzy, Charles shoved his rifle down her throat, choking her to death. Caril Ann was nonplussed. The only thing she could think of was to post a note to keep people away. She therefore taped a piece of paper to the front door, reading "Stay away, everybody is sick with the flu." And she walked away, leaving the bodies and Charles, and planted herself in the family room. She sat down and watched television. Psychiatrists agree that Caril Ann Fugate had been traumatized, shocked by this experience. While she watched TV, her boyfriend worked to conceal the bodies. During testimony, Starkweather insisted that "she was helping with all of it." Most experts agree this is not consistent with her profile.

Caril Ann was now also in a position to flee. But rather than rushing to begin their life on the lam, the couple stayed in the house and, according to Charles, "made love and watched TV, 'til we realized we didn't have any more food." And Caril Ann was afraid that a neighbor would check in on the family and discover her alone in the house, which would lead to questions about her family's whereabouts. On January 27, the couple set out on their own.

Charles' car stalled near a farm, the very next day. The farmer who owned the property, 70-year-old August Meyer, approached the car. Whatever pleasantry or challenge Mr. Meyer may have uttered, Charles replied in the language of the rifle, killing the old man — and his dog, to boot. Now, the young couple was in a hurry; there was no time to get the car re-started and free it from the mud, so they abandoned it. They made their way to a main road and hitchhiked on out of there.

Two teenagers, 17-year-old Robert Jensen and 16-year-old Carol King, noticed the pair and offered them a ride. The couple was terrified when Charles pulled out his rifle, forcing Robert to drive to an old, abandoned school. Profiler and psychiatrist Dr. Neil Gould points out that, at this juncture, "Charles' sociopathic tendencies begin to show: his thrill in taking life, his delight in his own power, probably almost euphoric, having never experienced his own sense of. . . dominance until now."

The crime that ensued bears out Dr. Gould's explanation. Until now, the crimes had been ignited by confrontation or, at least, had some slender motivation. Young Robert Colvert had been shot once through the head, most likely because Starkweather wanted to clear the robbery scene of witnesses. But with Carol King and Robert Jensen, his savagery escalated. First, he took the couple to the cellar of the building. He shot Robert Jensen six times in the head. Of course, he died instantly. Carol King witnessed the murder, and presumably feared the same for herself — never anticipating that she might suffer something even worse. Charles forced her to the ground and raped her. Then, removing himself from her body, he reached for his rifle and shot her while she was trying to pull herself together after this repulsive sexual act.

Charles claimed, in testimony, that Caril Ann became incensed — which is why Robert's genitals were mutilated: in a jealous rage, she cut up the boy's genitalia. Again, most experts still maintain that Caril Ann Fugate stood by, witnessing all the brutal events in a state of trauma, held hostage by her fear of this man; Starkweather almost certainly mutilated Jensen himself.

The bodies were left in the school's cellar, while Caril Ann and Charles fled in the young victims' car. Now we verge into the realm of speculation, as the testimonies differ. Starkweather has claimed that he was out of control, and needed to "turn himself in," maintaining that it was Fugate who fought against that possibility. In any event, the automobile found its way back to Lincoln, with both perpetrators still intact and moving forward. "I continued to be in fear for (my) life as a kidnapping victim of my lover," Caril Ann has said. That is easy to believe.

Back on familiar turf, Charles boasted that he knew how to get his hands on some "real" money. He took his child-lover to the home of the wealthy businessman, C. Lauer Ward. Breaking into the house, they surprised his wife, Clara, and Lillian Fencl, the maid. After binding the women at their wrists and ankles, he dragged them into a bedroom. This time, he used a different weapon, exhibiting his fascination and excitement with brutality. The women were stabbed to death, while Caril Ann stayed in another room.

Charles then joined her, and they waited for Mr. Ward to come home. Sometime that evening, hours after the initial break-in, the man let himself into his house — to be greeted by gunfire, instead of his wife. He was killed immediately. The date was January 30, 1958. By now, Caril Ann's family had been found, and members of the Nebraska National Guard and other law enforcement officials were attempting to track the couple. Unfortunately, they were unsuccessful for several fatal days.

Caril Ann and Charles took the Ward's limousine and drove toward Washington State. By February 1, they arrived in Douglas, Wyoming. Obviously, the limousine was too conspicuous, so Charles decided to steal a less assuming vehicle. Luck was on his side: they came upon a salesman who had pulled over to catch a quick nap. He slept through Charles' attack, sliding straight from a nap into death.

Merle Collison was dragged from his car, but not before a motorist stopped at the scene to lend assistance, assuming there had been an accident. Without a word, Charles pulled out his trusty gun. This time, luck went the other way: the unsuspecting Samaritan was quick, and grabbed for the rifle, himself. As the two men struggled, a deputy sheriff drove past. He quickly re-approached the scene; and Caril Ann Fugate ran toward him, screaming, "He killed a man!" The officer reached for his pistol. Charles jumped into the limousine and was off again — this time, alone. But for a very brief time: after a high-speed chase, several dozen police officers caught up with him, and finally, even Charles recognized he wouldn't be able to shoot his way out. He gave in.

Is this a story of mutual guilt, or sociopath and victim? Eleven lives were taken in this wave of terror, beginning with Caril Ann's own family. Charles maintained that it was always Caril Ann who insisted they continue pressing on, while he had decided at the school to "turn (myself) in." The jury's decision shows that they were inclined in favor of Caril Ann's version of events: Charles was given the death penalty and Fugate received a life sentence.

Charles Starkweather went to the electric chair on June 24, 1959, in Nebraska State Prison.

Caril Ann Fugate began her sentence at a women's correctional facility in Nebraska. After a few years, corrections officers and other prison officials were describing the inmate in the same terms her friends had used when she was no more than a child — sincere, friendly, and trustworthy. Indeed, her genuine sense of remorse for the 1958 crime spree (while adamantly denying her complicity) earned an almost universal empathy. She was paroled after almost two decades, in 1976. The warden of her prison was one of her strongest supporters. Now, forty years after the gruesome events, she still maintains her innocence.

To date, no one knows for certain to what degree Caril Ann Fugate was involved in the 1958 murders. Most believe she innocently fell under the "spell" of an older male, as so many girls do, at one time or another. That Charles was a sociopath created an unexpected and unthinkable version of "young love." Caril Ann's testimony is consistent with the facts derived from the crime scenes. And given the generalized profile of male/female serial-killing teams, which are mostly dominated by an aggressive (and murderous) male, it is much more likely that Charles Starkweather was the primary (if not sole) source of brutality and murder. And while both the specific evidence and the general suggestions of criminal profiling lead most to believe that Fugate was hostage to a killer, not a willing participant, that does not mitigate the horrific results of this appalling month, so heinous that it remains one of the most frightening cases in American history.

Ian Brady, born in 1938, spent most of his childhood in foster care. His Scottish mother, a cocktail waitress, lived a disruptive life — she was too promiscuous, too dependent on alcohol to have custody of her son for any length of time. Ian expressed his anger by ignoring his mother or striking out at her, verbally, during her visits. Foster care proved unpredictable and often the conditions were less than acceptable; years later, Ian described that he felt he was "there for families to make money. Yet (I) saw the least of the grub, had fewer pieces of clothing. . . " He knew better than to lash out at the authorities as a youngster, but his rage built as the years went by, and he needed to vent, ultimately.

Early on, he began to take pleasure in torturing animals; breaking a small dog's hind legs; decapitating a cat; setting fire to one of his foster family's dogs. As an adolescent, his brutality escalated. He profoundly resented the "siblings" whose housing he had to share, always knowing that:

> My place was somewhere far outside the family. I never got on with the children, never felt they wanted me around. It wasn't my fault — but you can't continue to try and get along when they ignore you, make you feel as if you don't exist, really.

Perhaps it was this focused rage that suggested to him a new outlet: he began to hurt small children. This time, the authorities took serious notice, and so began Ian's life going in and out of institutions. When he was not spending time in juvenile reformatory, he continued to engage in acts of sadism and thievery, ultimately landing in a cell at Borstal.

Meanwhile, Myra Hindley was growing up. She was hardly a renowned academic, but she had a mild temperament and her life was quite unexceptional. Born in July, 1942, in Groton, England, she was sent to live with her grandmother at the age of four, when her sister was born and her mother deemed the house "overcrowded." She was very close to her grandmother, so the move was not traumatic. She had no criminal history — indeed, her childhood friends and neighbors recall her as "likeable" and "friendly." Myra never attended college and worked at menial jobs, but she was a devout Catholic, a regular churchgoer, apt in the history of her church and faithful to its teachings.

It was while working at Millwards Chemical Suppliers in 1961 that her path crossed with Ian Brady's. His "faith" in the Nazi philosophy was as strong as hers in Catholicism. His charm outweighed her religious conviction; soon, she was leaning toward his teachings, receiving his Nazi-sympathizer sermons as gospel. He was engrossed in his interest in the historical leaders of Nazi Germany and his devotion to fascism. Myra saw Ian as the man he liked think he was: brilliant, special. Finally, he took her to a movie about the Nuremberg war crimes trials. Self-conscious in her ignorance, Myra sat quietly beside Ian, attempting to understand not only the trials but his fascination. Her subservience delighted him. After this initial date, the two became inseparable. To 19-year-old Myra, the 23-year-old philosopher seemed not so much sadistic as enlightened. She was flattered to think that someone intelligent found her interesting. Her awareness of her lesser intelligence gnawed at her self-esteem; rather than ever disagree with Ian and display her idiocy, she habitually agreed with everything he believed in. As Ian rambled on with his theories about the rights of the Nazis, and the need to capture, torture and even kill the Jews, she listened, focusing on her attempts to participate in the conversation without revealing her inferiority.

When he introduced sado-sexual encounters to her, identifying that he wanted to "teach" her the ways of the Nazis, she submitted. His pleasure gave her satisfaction. Her lover seemed worldly and knowledgeable. She thought it best not to question. And in the next year, she became more desensitized to his often brutal ways, even considering their lifestyle loving and normal.

To further please Ian, Myra took up readings about the Marquis de Sade and other sadistic, historical figures. The two spent their weekends reading to each other, Ian gleeful at his mate's growing interest in his own fascinations. Myra forged a vicarious identity through the infamous Irma Grese, a female administrator of the Nazi concentration camp at Belsen, well-known for her sadism. In Myra's attempt to parallel the figure, she bleached her hair and began dressing in jackboots and black leather. Brady was thrilled, sexually and psychologically. He began to refer to her as "Myra Hess."

Myra was making little money as a clerk-typist for the chemical company. He made little more as a rep. Ian persuaded his lover to participate in his scheme to create pornographic movies for sale. Together, they engaged in a variety of sexual positionings, including bondage. The films didn't sell, but the couple had achieved a higher level of sexual fantasy. Performing on film had increased Ian's appetite for alternative sexual situations. Watching himself and Myra in bondage, on film, thrilled him.

Ian would sit on his enthusiasm until the night he went to see the docudrama, *Compulsion*. The story illustrates the lives of the infamous child murderers Loeb and Leopold. He took Myra to see the movie, and it became the core of most of their conversations. Ian pulled from the film that an act of murder was a demonstration of love. Myra predictably went along with Ian's fantasy — his escalating dream of murdering to create some sort of romantic statement to his lover.

But in 1963, it was no longer mere discussion — fantasy had developed into very real planning stages. Then, action: during the next two years, Myra Hindley and Ian Brady took the lives of at least five children, abducting, assaulting and murdering boys and girls whose ages ranged from ten to seventeen. Ironically, their first victim would be the last to be found.

On July 12, 1963, 16-year-old Pauline Reade disappeared. She lived a couple doors down from the house the Hindleys shared with Myra's grandmother, her sister Maureen and her brother-in-law, David Smith. Reade was last seen at her home. It would take twenty years to uncover her remains. Indeed, it was twenty years before a confession explained her disappearance and linked it to the couple.

Victim number two was 12-year-old John Kilbride. It was November 23, 1963. The boy was going home from a movie theater when Myra approached him, offering a ride. She was at the town market of Ashton-Under-Lyne — a safe-enough place, a normal-enough woman. The boy was never seen again; at least, not until October 21, 1965 when his body was recovered from Saddleworth Moor. An autopsy revealed sodomy, and semen around his mouth. It appears that he'd been forced to engage in oral copulation as well as other forms of brutality.

The couple's third victim was also 12 years old: Keith Bennett, on his way to spend the night with his grandmother, on the evening of June 16, 1964. Again, Myra and her unassuming demeanor worked to lure the youngster into a car. And like Kilbride, he was never seen again — indeed, even his body has never been recovered. In 1986 Myra confessed to his murder, but it has proven futile to search the moors, where she believes the body still lies, deep beneath the heath.

The next known victim disappeared on December 26, 1965. Lesley Ann Downey, 10, vanished while walking along the streets of Manchester. Not far from the grave of John Kilbride, her tiny body was found buried on Saddleworth Moor. She was discovered after a 10-month search. Though only limited forensics analyses were performed, again it was proven that a "Moor" victim had been raped and tortured prior to her murder. Her body was covered with wounds, including knife mutilations. Later, a videotape would be found, created by the duo during a torture session with the child, and her recorded screams, her pleas to be released, speak for themselves.

Finally, Ian and Myra were getting sloppy. Ian was so desensitized to his own heinous nature that he considered sharing his murder stories with his brother-in-law, David Smith, who shared their house. Ian had been a sort of hero to David, showing off his gun collection and bondage tools; the younger man had found his rebel nature entertaining. Ian had found Myra easy to persuade; he never doubted that his adoring in-law would be any different. Indeed, he was an easier target to pull into his murderous ventures — David already exhibited a criminal tendency, having been arrested a few times for theft, once for assault.

Ian spoke candidly of his private world with Myra, and the children they'd killed. The 18-year-old listened, considering such stories to be largely Ian's embellishments. When Ian offered to "indoctrinate" him into their clan, David went along, almost laughing. The men left the house, hopped in Ian's car and headed for a local pub. They struck up a conversation with a young homosexual, Edward Evans, 17, and after a few drinks, Evans agreed to leave with the men.

Back at Myra's house, Ian invited Edward into the sitting room, beckoning him to sit down on the couch. Ian left the room for an instant, leaving David to keep their new acquaintance company. Moments later, Ian was on the young guest, swinging at him with an axe. When David saw this, he was not amused — he was scared to death. "I felt I'd seen the Devil," he would later say. "He looks at me and tells me that it's a bloody mess, the bloodiest yet, that it isn't usually more than a single blow." Edward Evans died on October 6, 1965.

While another youngster succumbed to Ian's evil, police were only beginning to suspect that they had a serial killer on their hands. They had no witnesses, no solid forensic evidence; they could only assume that the cases had been unrelated — until the count passed three. As Myra and Ian read about the missing children, a feeling of power surged through them as they realized how invincible they were. They'd gone nearly two years undetected. The spree might have continued, but David, the supposed new "member" of the killing team, spoke up.

David went to the police sometime that evening, after witnessing the crime. "He told me to help him as he swung that hatchet. The boy had no idea. I must say he was trying to stay alive, and Ian was yelling to me to help him, but I couldn't, I couldn't move." His confession coincided with a rather different conversation taking place between Myra and Ian. No longer satiated with children, Ian wanted to try new ideas in their killing routine. Couples? Women? He wasn't exactly sure; he only knew that he was getting tired of repeating the same scenario.

When a knock came on the door, interrupting his latest

"vision," Myra welcomed the police who only minutely caught her off guard. With Ian's self-confidence to reassure her, Myra felt superior, offering tea and coffee while Edward's body lay in a bloody heap in her bedroom. The police searched the house, finding the body within minutes. On October 7, 1965, Myra Hindley and Ian Brady were taken into custody.

David continued to assist the police. He mentioned a locker, located at Manchester Central Station. Inside there were two suitcases filled with nude photos, mostly of their female victims. There was some rope, wire and chain, handcuffs and knives. Most important to the trial, the tape of little Leslie's cries for help, pleas for release. There were also snapshots of Saddleworth Moor; the authorities now had all they needed to confirm their belief that these perpetrators were also responsible for the bodies found at that location.

The media took hold of the case, dubbing it the "Moors Murders," comparing it to Jack the Ripper in England's history of grisly murders. The trial came to be known as the "trial of the century." And while it was short, it still stands as one of England's most infamous. The jury could hardly listen to the tape, some of the members crying as they witnessed the gruesome torture session.

On May 6, 1966, the couple was found guilty; both were sentenced to the maximum for their crimes: life without possibility of parole.

In 1986, Keith Bennett's mother wrote to Myra. Until that missive, she had never disclosed the truth, never confessed to any crime. But she was moved by the letter, and decided to assist the authorities in recovering bodies as well as providing more intimate details of the crimes, and the crime scenes. Detective Chief Superintendent Peter Topping had stayed with the case for over two decades, still searching for Keith and Pauline Reade. Myra was successful in leading him to Pauline but, sadly, Bennett's body still rests in the Moors.

Today, Ian lives his life within the confines of an institution for the mentally insane; he was diagnosed schizophrenic shortly after his sentencing. He has never asked for release. By contrast, Myra claims she has gone back to Catholicism; further, she has "experienced a religious conversion." She pleads with the British Home Secretary for release. To date, her wishes have been denied. She continues to serve her sentence at the Durham Prison for Women.

## JUDITH ANN AND ALVIN NEELLEY

Judith Ann Neelley and her husband Alvin committed some fifteen murders, most of them sexual, most of them against girls or women, cutting cross a swath of territory from Alabama to Georgia and Tennessee.

Judith was born in 1963. The crime spree is believed to have begun in 1982, although some unsolved cases occurring as early as 1980 are thought to have been the work of the Neelleys. Judith was a decade younger than her husband; she was only 19 when the two met. She was Alvin's second wife. No one is sure whether Judith was fully aware of her husband's nature or history when she married him; most experts are certain, however, that she easily adjusted to him and his lifestyle.

Alvin had a long history of abuse and brutality toward women, particularly, and had already served time in prison for shooting and critically injuring his first wife. He was 24 at the time of that attempted murder.

In all cases of male/female team crime, a critical question is the

woman's predisposition to be dominated. That may be a lesser factor in the current example (although experts assume she was also a
battered woman), for it seems that Judith was quite comfortable
looking at the victims as a way to satiate her husband's compulsive
need to commit violent acts.

Alvin maintains that Judith took the lead in organizing the
murders. Judith did have a criminal history, herself, unlike the profile of most team-killer females, and there is adequate reason to believe that in this instance a parallel pathology was at work in both
their minds.

Judith is believed to have shot a man, while she was in her
teens; she got away with that one. Then she committed armed robbery with her husband, and both were incarcerated. During her jail
term, she gave birth to twins. Her husband and she were released in
early 1982. Free again, tied down by neither a job nor, apparently, by
their children, they drifted aimlessly through the southern states. In
that year, they began to rob again and commit other crimes — minor assaults, stolen vehicles and petty theft.

And while the first murder to be examined was not, most
likely, the first they committed, it is exemplary in revealing the roles
each one played, and especially, Judith's (unconscious?) desire to be
caught.

On September 25, 1982, the Neelleys were cruising a popular
mall in Rome, Georgia, looking for a victim. They found her in 13-
year-old Lisa Millican, who had chosen the wrong day to go out
shopping. They kidnapped the child and drove her to a motel room,
where she was molested for several days; the twins looked on. After
about a week, Judith attempted to kill the girl by injecting her with
drain cleaner — but she survived. Infuriated, the couple drove her to
a rural area in Alabama, shot her several times, and dumped her
body in the river.

After the Millican murder, Judith began acting out of character, which proved pivotal in the couple's arrest. Judith made a series of phone calls to the police, directing them to the victim's body. Every time she called, she was recorded; however, her voice went unidentified. While the authorities were trying to find both the perpetrator and the body (at this point, they assumed one killer), the team struck again.

In Rome, Georgia, Judith casually introduced herself to a young couple, inviting them to "party" in the late afternoon. John Hancock, 26, took his girlfriend, Janice Chapman, 23, along for a ride with their new "friend." They drove to an isolated area outside of town, and when they arrived, Judith introduced them to Alvin. They were talking casually, but when John turned his back, Alvin took out his gun and shot him in the back. They assumed he was dead and moved on to Janice, whom they raped repeatedly and then shot. They thought they'd left no living witnesses, but Hancock survived his wounds; he was able to provide a lucid description of the suspects.

The crime paralleled Judith's phoned-in description of the murder of Lisa Millican. Detectives asked John to listen to the recorded voice; he recognized Judith immediately. The authorities now knew they were tracking two persons, and they had a description of both, as well as of the vehicle that Judith had used to drive John and Janice to the "party scene."

Sketches were distributed to several state police divisions, and many authorities distributed copies randomly so that, in Tennessee, a clerk identified the killers while they were attempting to cash what turned out to be a bad check. She called the police. With John Hancock coming along to confirm the identities, the police moved to the check-cashing office. Hancock identified the assailants immediately, and they were taken into custody.

Under interrogation, Alvin claimed that Judith had been the mastermind. Meanwhile, Judith claimed she was the battered victim of a sex-crazed monster. She felt she had no option but to help him carry out his plans.

John Hancock's role, at this juncture, was as important as it had been in locating the killers. Who was telling the truth? According to John, ultimately Judith had been equally brutal, matching her husband's rage against young Janice. What, then, had led her to act in the way she did — making revealing phone calls? Prosecutors and law enforcement officials agreed that Judith Neelley had taken an active role in many, perhaps all, of the murders perpetrated by the couple.

Alvin Neelley pled guilty to two counts of murder in Georgia and received two life sentences. A jury of his peers found him guilty. Judith Neelley went to trial for murder in Alabama (for Lisa Millican) and the jury sentenced her to death; the judge overruled that, sentencing her to life imprisonment.

CAROL BUNDY AND DOUGLAS CLARK

After my first book (on male sexual predators and serial killers) was released, in 1998, I was interviewed for a television program. I had agreed with the show's producers that they could contact subjects of their choice, from the pages in my book — and indeed, at the show's initiative, several of the men agreed to phone
in — Douglas Clark included.

For two years I had corresponded with the "Sunset Slayer,"
who is on death row for his part in the murders of several Los Angeles prostitutes during the early 1980s. Douglas is incredibly tricky. It
is not uncommon for serial killers to use God as part of an effort to
feign an otherwise wholesome attitude about life, and to justify or
attempt to discount their crimes. Some serial killers will make attempts to overcome their crimes through a "religious conversion." In
other words, while some killers are profoundly repentant, many use
religion or otherwise "positive" lifestyle characteristics to suggest
that over all, they are not deviant. They hope, by this, to gain sympa-

thy from both the jury and the media, and therefore to reap lesser sentences for their actions. But Douglas is unique in his slant on his own profile.

He plays into his perversity, claiming it is his nature to be highly sexual — yes, even deviant. But how did that make him a killer?, Douglas will ask, more concerned and incredulous than anyone. His argument is quite simple: he loves women, and sex in every form, and has no hang-ups with "alternative sex," which he referred to in his letters (to me) as "threesomes, infidelities and lesbianism." In fact, he went out of his way to let me know that he was anything but afraid to say that my letters excited him; he was lonely and hungry for a woman, and just thinking about me, "at my computer, [him] between my legs. . . " Well, the point is, his ploy is to show that he has nothing to be ashamed of, he isn't hiding anything, not his love of women, sex, or even his outrageous comments bordering on perversity.

In portraying himself as an honest, lustful man, he is attempting to discount everyone's assumption that he has anything to repress; that it was his lover, Carol Bundy, who has psychological issues — instabilities that would ultimately lead to murder — and that she kept more secrets about her own deviant sex life than anyone he claims to have ever been involved with: so that she, obviously, is the killer. "Her rage, and her sex drive. . . she is so out of touch with her needs. She is locked up, within. Not just behind bars. But inside. She always was. It led to an anger so deep. . . twisted jealousies. . . that's why she killed — not just the women, but her own boyfriend." I had to admit, his argument was a masterful example of manipulation.

In fact, I had grown accustomed to three categories of killers — those who confess, those who "can't talk about it because it's between [him] and God," and those who deny everything completely. But Doug had etched out his own fascinating slant. On some level, there was a logic to his argument. Indeed, why would he have to kill, or conceal his actions — or his victims' bodies — when he was so flamboyantly *not* repressed? It was Carol, he pointed out, who was always skirting the issues, trying to cadge money or other personal gain. While I didn't take Doug seriously, I began to see how (if he treated all women with the same candid ardor) he might seem attractive to the unsuspecting; take that one step further, and he might seem heaven-sent to less-alluring candidates like Carol. Yet Doug was cavalier about it all, from the get-go, and it was Carol who had broken, and confessed. It was she who had led investigators to the head in the freezer and the nude photos of little girls, back at the lovers' apartment.

And then, on this particular TV program, Doug called in. The scene had already been set, with a description similar to that which I've provided above. Much to my surprise, when Doug came on the telephone, the energy he exuded in his letters was absent. His voice was quiet, sullen. He described me as "a lonely housewife who [he'd] taken great measures to try and provide some color for." I sat listening, and realized once again how incredibly cunning these predators are. They don multiple masks, depending on the audience. For the show, he was an articulate man drawing parallels between me, in many ways, and his pathological lover, Carol. I, too, "suffered isolation and intense loneliness. [He] had taken the grave responsibility of trying to help me with my 'self-esteem issues'."

I got through the interview, only momentarily thrown off by this new identity emerging before me, and quickly decided that I needed to deal more patiently with Carol. She was not willing to speak with me, not for a very long time. . . I considered her life with this man, and his many masks — aggressive, intimidating, sexual, sarcastic, impressive, charming. . . I needed to find out more about her life as a team killer with Doug. Only Carol had real information about the true workings of all those forms of manipulation that create a submissive accomplice.

But I never got too far with Carol. I think of her as someone who, emotionally, dissipated altogether. Even in reference to her children, she remains monotone, and the prospect of never hearing from her two sons (both having been subjected to her bizarre life with Doug) doesn't trigger any more emotion than Doug's perversities.

Carol's example allows specific questions of sanity to be brought to the forefront. She is at once "extremely fearful of Doug, never knowing what he'll do to her. . . " and "warm and fuzzy because [he] sent [me] a teddy bear," (which isn't possible, to begin with). Her own statements demand we take a closer look at her ability to assess truth and reality.

When I had finished researching both of them, I received a letter from a woman who is not that different from myself, just a few years my junior. Also engaged in research, she may differ from me only in that she has come to believe in Douglas, which is proof that his manipulations are not only a window into the mind and the workings of a killer, but that even academics are persuaded:

> *Dear Jennifer,*
>
> *I have been in contact with Doug for three years. I have seen his transcripts and have been informed that you also have read them. How could experts be so stupid? I'm a criminology major and went into this research considering Doug Clark guilty. Now, after coming to know him as I do, as well as many of his friends on the outside who support him and still work toward financially aiding him in his appeals process, I can't help but feel utterly shocked by this system! When I graduate, I will be a profiler. I will do what I can to help Doug Clark receive a fair trial. If you would like to contact me, feel free. I think all of Doug's friends should stay in contact.*
>
> *Yours,*
>
> *(Name withheld)*

The point of sending me the letter was twofold: Douglas was letting me know that he'd discussed me with others, even provided personal information like my mailing address. He had that power. Secondly, he was assuring me that I'd "better not be a bad girl," as he'd frequently joked with me, with an underlying threat. . . and do anything or say anything that might "piss off one of [his] many fans."

It is a surreal experience, trying to communicate with these two lust killers. There is no sign of remorse on Doug's part, and we still see glimpses of Carol's need to be loved by Douglas — at any cost, including the loss of her life to prison, or the loss of her children's love.

Douglas Clark "taught" me that the power of the team killer to persuade an accomplice is unlimited; indeed, this sort of manipulative personality can control on a universal level. Men like Clark use their powers not only to persuade the Carol Bundys — the lonely, frumpy women hungry for affection — but as the letter from the young researcher proves, academics can fall victim as well.

Carol still comes across as halfhearted when it comes to her own assessments of her life with Douglas — that is, when she's willing to speak of her life of crime at all. Mostly, she discusses her health, her need for money, and her disgust with the prison and its unfair treatment of inmates with disabilities. They both make it clear that they are very far from recognizing the reality of their heinous actions, and one can only conclude that they would start up again, if the opportunity ever arose.

Carol Bundy moved into a small apartment complex in Los Angeles in January of 1979. She was a newly divorced mother of two. At 36, she was already suffering from severe diabetes, cataracts, and obesity. While her ex-husband had been psychically abusive during the most of their almost decade-long marriage, Carol had no record of criminal activity or spousal abuse. Her new life in her new apartment was small, literally and figuratively. With her health problems, her job opportunities seemed limited and her space, shared with a 5 year old and an 8 year old, was barely large enough. John Murray, the landlord at her complex, became her "savior" of sorts. He helped her increase her Social Security by $620, and got her a cane, and even a job — he combed the want ads, promoting her employability as a nurse (which was her vocation).

Bundy was hardly the kind of attractive young divorcee that married men sometimes fall for, and there is still speculation as to what Mr. Murray saw in Ms. Bundy, beyond a sincere desire to help a young, needy mother. As an immigrant from Australia, Murray seemed to empathize with her efforts to start over. He definitely took on the role of hero. He helped her in many ways, and, all things considered, he increased her self-esteem. Within months of their initial meeting, they had become lovers.

For Carol, it was "love;" for John, it was simply an "affair." A married man with several children, he was unwilling to meet Carol's ultimate expectation — a monogamous relationship. Carol was certain that John Murray stayed in the relationship with his wife out of duty, not love. She confronted his wife with $1500 in cash and a threat that she'd better "leave." The only thing this scheme accomplished was to drive John back to his own family, away from Carol and the conflict the affair created.

She saw little of John around the complex after that; he went to great lengths to avoid her. When Carol called needing a handyman, John made sure that she was out before he stepped in to address her plumbing or other complaints. Carol was devastated by the rejection. She did not let pride come between her and her man. If he would not meet her, then she would go out and find him.

John had a part-time job as a country singer in North Hollywood at a country-western nightclub called Little Nashville. Carol made the bar her regular hangout. John continued to ignore his ex-lover's swooning, but her nights at the club would prove surprisingly fruitful. A dashing man five years her junior began a flirtatious courtship with "Plain Jane." Douglas Daniel Clark already had a reputation at the bar for his fast and loose lifestyle. He wasn't known for being particular about his sex-mates; indeed, he often approached lonely, less attractive women like Bundy, because they proved to be a financial pay-off: free drinks, clothes, even a place to stay. Doug immediately spotted Carol's neediness and vulnerability, and just as fast, he took advantage. Within weeks, he was not ashamed or afraid to share his dreams with his latest lover — including rape, torture and murder. Carol thought all of his talk was just fantasy. After such musings, however, Doug would engage her in heated sex; and his attention made her feel like a school girl, on top of the world. Carol came to recognize Doug's discussion of murder and mayhem as his aphrodisiac, a prelude to sex. In turn, she received fulfillment and gratification, through his excitement displaced unto her.

And while Clark was a mechanic by trade, and less-educated than Bundy, he was the son of a Navy admiral with many stories to share. He was unusually articulate. Indeed, in a matter of weeks, the younger man was articulating his way into her apartment. In the back of Carol Bundy's mind, John Murray still took first place. She tried to concentrate on Doug and have him replace John in her thoughts, but the pride he had allowed her was diminishing, as his fantasy discussions of bringing other girls into their sex life were becoming more serious talk. "I was incredibly fragile. I didn't know if I could lose Doug, but I had no idea he was capable of murder."

Carol allowed Doug his discussions, secretly feeling jealous and insecure; more than that, she was afraid of being rejected by another man. Carol had anticipated that, living together, they would have less need to talk about extra-curricular activities since they'd be together, most of the time, to fulfill each other's needs. As a footnote, she prayed she was making John Murray jealous. On both counts, Carol was wrong.

Once Doug Clark moved in, John was relieved, able to go back to his family without feeling stalked — or guilty. And once Doug moved in, Doug himself went from being gallant and charming to controlling. Soon, Carol was responsible for all the household chores, including his laundry and dishes, as well as play-acting the role of sex slave to keep her man happy. Once again, Bundy was giving in to Clark, becoming more his puppet in hopes that she would be enough to satisfy him. If he needed bondage or slavery role-playing, she would oblige — anything, for his monogamy in return.

Clark was not amused that the Bundy "package" included children. He was abusive, and when the boys attempted to argue with him or tell their mother what he had done, Clark would beat them; once, he pulled a knife on the elder son. The children went to their mother in utter fear. But Bundy believed that the boys weren't in any danger, explaining, "He wasn't a homosexual."

This concept of fear, related solely to sex, was probably based on her experience with Doug and an 11-year-old girl neighbor. In the early 1980s, the child was lured into their apartment, coerced into showering with both adults and then photographed, nude. On top of everything else, Clark was a pedophile. "I realized this was bad. I didn't feel competitive, because she was a child. I suppose I knew it was wrong." Clark had introduced Bundy into his dark world, complete with bondage, slavery, child abuse and pedophilia. By mid-1980, he would introduce her to murder.

The couple began cruising LA boulevards in search of victims. On June 11, 1980, Cynthia Chandler, 16, and her half-sister, Gina Mirano, were both abducted at Huntington Beach. They were found the next day near the Ventura Highway, next to Sunset Boulevard in Griffith Park. The girls had been forced to perform fellatio; while doing so, they were shot through the head. The media pounced on the news, dubbing a potential serial killer the Sunset Slayer. No one guessed that he wasn't working alone. No one would believe, later, that he'd been working with a woman.

On June 24, 1980, a prostitute in her early 20s was found dead behind a restaurant. Karen Jones had been shot in the head. The same day, in Studio City, a headless corpse was found. Later it was determined to be the body of 20-year-old prostitute Exile Wilson.

Doug loved this life. His sex slave was also his lure. She had all but rid herself of her children, who had begged to move in with relatives. Doug had free range throughout the apartment. He went so far as to preserve Exxie Wilson's head in the freezer — he was also a necrophiliac. Carol has confessed to keeping Exxie's head in the freezer, freshly made-up at all times, so that it was available and satisfying when Doug asked for it. He would call her to bring it to him in the shower, where he would perform necrophilic fellatio.

As heinous as Bundy's actions were, the question remains, "Why?" Carol Bundy had no previous criminal record — sexual or otherwise. A divorced mother of two, she was a lonely woman searching for a loving relationship. She became, in the eyes of a righteous society, evil. However, a broader inquiry into this subject must go beyond blanket statements that mask an entire subculture of killers. We must learn why a woman can be persuaded to cross the limits and perform such deeds — for a specific man, a killer. Should we categorize her as a victim of her abuser — or as a lust killer, herself?

Still, no one knew, or suspected, about Carol. Other bodies were found along Sunset Boulevard. Two hitchhikers were found near Malibu — all pattern killings, linked by a .38 pistol shot to the head. Carol was weakening. Doug's escapades were finally catching up with her psyche. Her role in the crimes rested with Doug; she showed no propensity for violence, on her own. "I can't remember my mother more than spanking me — and rarely," says Carol's son, "until Doug. Even then, she didn't hurt me; it's what she allowed to happen, what she allowed him to do to us. We lived in Hell."

Carol drove to Burbank, to the Little Nashville. On August 5, she took John Murray aside and confessed to him what she had become involved in. Seeing the horror on John's face, she immediately regretted telling him. She told him to meet her around midnight, at his van, parked in the club's lot. Unable to take back her words, she chose to remedy her slip by murdering John. In a savage surprise attack, she stabbed him several times, cutting off a chunk of his buttocks and, finally, decapitating him. She jumped in her station wagon — with the head, assuming it would hold cops from identification for a few days while she "sorted stuff out." She threw the head in a ravine, and to date, it remains undiscovered.

A week later, at the same job John had helped her to land, she confessed to her killing spree in collaboration with Clark. She seemed to be having a breakdown, but one woman took her seriously enough to notify the authorities. Clark was shocked when police met him at the boiler room where he was employed. He is still "shocked." In his words, "Carol is a lesbian-dike-bitch who killed with her boy-toy-Murray, then killed him." He's just a victim with a death sentence.

The .38 caliber pistol used in the crimes proved to be Clark's, and was the key weapon during trial. The gun and Carol's testimony proved sufficient to put Doug away; the head in the freezer and nude photos of a child — with his fingerprints — helped.

In 1983, Douglas Daniel Clark was charged guilty on multiple counts of homicide, and subsequently sentenced to death. He is currently on death row at San Quentin. Carol Bundy received multiple and consecutive prison terms ranging from 25 years to life imprisonment (with the possibility of parole), which she serves at a California facility for women.

While Carol Bundy is classified as a "lust killer," she illustrates the ambiguous nature of "sanity." Within the United States, there is no model besides the McNaughton standard by which to base a judgment whether the accused's mental capacity is worthy of the court process. There is incredible disdain, most likely bred of the fear engendered by these unspeakable crimes, that prohibits most juries from discounting serial killings as acts of insanity. To establish a defense on this ground, it must be clearly proven that the party was laboring under a defect of reason from disease of the mind, not realizing the nature and quality of the act, or if he did know it, that (he) did not know he was doing what was wrong. This is founded in the analysis of the case brought against Daniel McNaughton, who on January 20, 1843, shot and killed the private secretary to the Prime Minister of England. The perpetrator suffered from psychological disorders and had been experiencing delusions for some time. Today, his behavior would be classified as schizophrenic. He was found not guilty by reason of insanity — a benchmark decision that has influenced the Western practice of law. It still holds as the model for cases of insanity pleas. And while it is clear that, in most cases of serial crime, sanity is proven, many experts within the legal system agree that the McNaughton test is not the only applicable standard to define "sanity." Certainly, serial crime is so heinous in itself, the perpetrators' mental state must be considered questionable, at best. In other words, serial crime brings with it much more complex disorders by which to judge capacity. Many of the behaviors that lead to serial crime, especially with women, have been labeled as disorders: Munchausen Syndrome by proxy, for example. A disorder is not the same as insanity, but when it leads to such extreme conduct as murder, has it not crossed a line?

When we look at murder, especially serial cases, juries have a hard time allowing for a plea of insanity. The punishments are less harsh, and there is room for the possibility of institutionalization rather than imprisonment or execution. This places a tremendous responsibility on our citizens. Society sets standards that we find reassuring: people who act out so gruesomely must be punished harshly. Any other choice but to find the culprit sane might allow a lesser sentence. The juror becomes intimately involved in determining the fate of an appalling killer, and with this comes the perspective that he is showing compassion if he is not severe. Carol Bundy's actions are unconscionable by most counts. She bargains for money and threatens anyone who she feels is a threat to her — even if that perceived emotional threat exists in her mind, alone. She is a danger to others. But is she sane?

By the United State's standards, the answer is yes, but some experts disagree. Her judgment is skewed and is based in unrealistic perceptions of both love and the degree of pain she inflicts on victims and their families, as well as her on own offspring. Still, while she is a poster woman personifying the question of insanity, she is typical of serial killers in her judgments and the vehement tendencies born of fantasies ignited by love or some other perceived personal benefit. Would it not be right, then, to segregate this classification of killers, as has been done within the FBI and psychological research organizations at Quantico, within the penal system as well? This provides an alternative that may appear reasonable, to some, and too forgiving to others. We have a social fear of letting serial killers "off the hook" by allowing them separate standards. But indeed, we may be doing a service if we let our experts reasonably explore the hypothesis that these people require a penal code all their own. They are incomparable to any other subculture of criminals in the world. And they are on the rise, due to our lack of understanding of the phenomenon.

## CHARLENE AND GERALD GALLEGO

The so-called Sex Slave Murders took the lives of at least ten women and men in California, Oregon and Nevada, where authorities were unable to apprehend the culprits for a tragically long time.

Gerald and Charlene Gallego started down their bloody road in 1978, in a spree that resulted in brutal sexual homicides that kept on happening until 1980. This team seems to have had a compulsive intent to collect sexual slaves — obviously to serve the perverse pleasures of the primary figure, Gerald, who was later acknowledged as the dominant figure as well as the sole actual murderer in the case.

Gerald Gallego was born in 1946. He followed in his father's footsteps. And his father was incarcerated at San Quentin when Gerald Jr. was born; he was serving time in Mississippi nine years later for two murders (one victim was a prison guard). In 1955, at the age of 28, Gerald Sr. received death by electrocution for the killings.

George Sr.'s wife attempted to protect their son from his reputation and from his example; she told young Gerald that his father was killed in an auto accident. In spite of her efforts, the boy seemed fated to repeat his father's brutal history. By the age of 12, he had been arrested for sexually molesting a 6-year- old girl in his Mississippi neighborhood, and he started toying with minor assaults and petty theft.

By his late 20s, Gerald Jr. had been married seven times, not always taking the trouble to divorce before marrying again. Known as a bigamist, by his early 30s he was fleeing Mississippi, trailing a series of charges including assault, incest and other sex crimes.

In a blatant contrast to Gerald Gallego, his last wife, Charlene, had been a quiet, seemingly well-adjusted child who attended church and school regularly. She had no history of crime, violence or abuse in any regard. But she gave herself over to Gerald; she seemed willing to follow in his perversities, which evolved into the criminal activity that began to spew from him like a volcano.

Gerald's murders were the result of his drive to dominate, violate, and ultimately possess girls: sex slaves. His fantasy was to collect young girls — virgins — who would be forced to look to him as their sole sexual mate, performing favors on demand, anything he asked. He explained to his wife that, to become erect, he had to have other women, and in complete subservience, at that. Further, his history of bigamy was related to this impotency; he could not become excited by a single woman.

As bizarre as it sounds, Charlene accepted his claims and, having been promised that this would "cure" his sex problem, she began to play a pivotal role in helping him lure in, then brutalize, young girls. Indeed, he never would have been as successful without her, in his kidnappings. Charlene's demeanor was likeable, soft, even soothing. Her stature, small and lithe, was completely unthreatening. Young girls innocently went with her, alone, back to the car, when she offered a joint or a beer.

On November 1, 1978, Tippi Vaught, 16, and Rhonda Scheffler, 17, willingly left a shopping center in Sacramento, California with Charlene. In Gerald's van, both girls were molested, beaten, then forced out, turned away and shot, execution-style. The bodies were found in the small rural area of Baxter.

In June, the following year, another pair of teen females vanished from a fairground in Reno, Nevada. Linda Judd was 14, her friend, Sandra Colley was 13. They were seduced by an offer of pot. For the three years that followed, the girls were considered "missing." In a later statement, Charlene would confess that they, too, had been their victims.

In spring 1980, the couple abducted teens from another shopping mall, also in Reno. Karen Chipman and Stacy Redican were found three months later. They'd met the same fate: sexual molestation, and then death by shooting.

The next abduction broke the pattern. Linda Aquilar was alone, pregnant, and a bit older — 21. The profile of the abduction changed, and the violence and means of death escalated. She was taken off a public street in June, in Oregon. She was beaten, raped, then suffocated by being buried alive outside the serene coastal area of Gold Beach.

A month later, Virginia Mochel, 34, was kidnapped from a Sacramento parking lot. She was married, a mother, and working as a bartender in a downtown pub. She never made it to her car. Virginia was forced to go with Gerald. Three months later her body was discovered, indicating strangulation after rape.

In November, Craig Miller and Beth Sower, a couple in their 20s, were kidnapped. Students at a Sacramento college, they'd been to a local fraternity dance; they were last seen by friends, apparently engaged in an argument inside a van with people who were not unidentified. A friend actually wrote down the license plate number, but didn't contact the police — yet. A day later, Craig's body was found, dumped alongside an isolated road. His fiancée had been forced to witness his execution. Afterwards, she was taken to a hotel and, while, Charlene sat in the front room, Gerald raped the terrified young woman throughout the night. The following morning, the couple drove her to a rural area, where Gallego shot her, too, in the back of the head. Charlene describes "hearing the cries. . . quiet, helpless moans from that young girl. . . "

Craig's friends heard on the news that his body had been found; they called the police with the license number, which touched off an intense manhunt. All the while, Charlene was leaving manic phone calls with her folks, which were traced as she and Gerald made their way to the Midwest. Federal agents tracked down the Gallegos in Omaha, Nebraska. The calls that had revealed their whereabouts were filled with shock, terror and remorse.

For eighteen months, delays and legal maneuvers kept the couple out of court. The trial date was quickly approaching — finally, in 1982, the day came. Suddenly, Charlene agreed to testify against her husband on the outstanding murder charges.

In the cases of Miller and Sower, Gerald was charged with two counts of murder and two counts of kidnapping. He was sentenced to death by electrocution.

In April, 1983, on trial for the kidnapping of Chipman and Redican in Nevada, Gerald Gallego again received the death penalty — by lethal injection.

Charlene agreed to become the main witness against her husband in his 1983 trial. She also waived extradition and returned to California, without question, to face her own destiny. For her cooperation with the authorities, Charlene Gallego received a reduced sentence of sixteen years and eight months for her part in the murders. It was clear from the evidence that Charlene was not physically involved in the murders (forensics officers found only Gerald's

DNA on the gun and gun powder; they found his pubic hairs and semen as well; but nowhere on any of the victims' bodies was there a link to Charlene. Today, Gerald sits on death row in Nevada, with appeals pending. Charlene has been released.

We continue to search for all the reasons why a person might become deviant, inexplicably violent. Looking at the case of Martha Beck and her later relationship with Raymond Fernandez, it is impossible not to factor in her childhood, and those events in her upbringing that may have played a role in driving her into a life of mayhem and sexual pathology.

Born Martha Seagrum, in 1920, she was raped by her brother at age 13. Perhaps in response to his sexual attack, she allowed herself to grow prodigiously fat. In a bizarre dichotomy, while she tried to elude his advances, her own sexual appetite grew — a longing for romance — but the damage was done: her gratification came from violent encounters. Martha confused sex and romance with rage and violence.

Martha's brother left home the year she graduated from high school. She was no longer a victim of repeated rape, but she appears to have become embittered about life and about emotional liaisons altogether. After graduation, she trained as a nurse and went to work as an undertaker's assistant. Her morbid surroundings only added to her sense that life held little meaning, and deserved little respect. The more she worked around death, the less affected she was by lifelessness. Her only remark about how her life experiences had affected her came out during trial: "In a bizarre fashion, I was learning something about disconnecting through my observations of death."

She did need love and emotional satisfaction, but on the surface she could not demonstrate this desire. Her supervisor described her, during testimony, as "cold, but hard-working, and always very. . . inward." In reality, Martha tried not to need anyone; she was trying desperately to learn about aloneness through the dead, all the while starving for personal relations.

She was in perfect form for Raymond Fernandez — a tragic pairing that would come a few years later.

She was appointed superintendent of a home for crippled children at Pensacola, Florida, in 1944. That same year, she married her third husband, Alfred Beck. They divorced within the year. She was 24. Her many failed relationships reflect her inability to bond with men.

Raymond Fernandez seemed equally disconnected from the human race and from the world of emotion. He was six years older than Martha, bringing to their eventual union a history that demonstrates his own inability to bond. Born in Hawaii, of Spanish descent, he had met and married a woman in Connecticut; he had four children with her, but when the fourth child was born, he split, abandoning his family without warning or rationale.

No one is sure how Raymond Fernandez ended up as a calculated killer. Some believe that an injury he suffered may have contributed to his devolution. During World War II, Fernandez served with the British Intelligence Service, honorably, but he suffered a head injury in 1945. It appeared to "unhinge" him, removing his inhibitions. He suddenly became fascinated with witchcraft, and claimed his Don Juan power over women had a psychic component. Maybe the women's adoration was real: he apparently went through about 100 women (and their bank accounts) in the year since he'd been discharged from service. His lovers and financial victims had been chosen from newspaper want ads, located under the heading the "Lonely Hearts Club," where he came to meet Martha Beck in 1947. She was certainly a "Lonely Heart," and so she had listed herself in an ad.

If, individually, their tales are fairly clear, the story becomes confusing after they came together. Psychologists agree that Martha's early sexual trauma had rendered her incapable of close, human bonding. In Raymond's case, there is agreement that due to the physiological impact of his accident, he was a "changed man." But the experts are powerless to explain what happened when they met. For whatever reason, they found some sort of connection with each other.

Martha weighed over 300 lbs; her weight seemed to moderate Raymond's sexual response, allowing him to befriend a woman, for once. She became his confidante. Friendship led to romance, and for Raymond it was stronger than he'd known before. He confessed to her his swindling ways. His frankness and sincerity allowed Martha to see that he was human. There were no false pretenses, even though what he was describing to her was illegal and unpalatable at best. She chose to view him as the most trustworthy man she'd met. And she finally allowed herself to fall in love. Besides, from the way he explained his lifestyle, she found this slight, somewhat handsome man exhilarating.

It wasn't long before they were scheming together. Unfortunately, Martha was jealous of the women who were Raymond's targets. Sexual pathology does not seem to have been a part of the couple's courtship, but murder ultimately played its part. Martha found herself frightened for the sanctity of their relationship, going to burlesque lengths to ensure Raymond's fidelity . . . in the end, she would kill to keep women at an extreme distance.

Raymond could not give up his cheating ways. He frequently fell from grace, and Martha's rage intensified.

In December 1948, Raymond met a widow from New York, the 66-year-old Janet Faye. She gave up most of her savings during the pseudo courtship and promises of marriage. One day, Raymond invited his "fiancée" to his apartment in Long Island, which he claimed to share with his "sister." Her death was brutal. He bludgeoned her to death, while Martha strangled her weak body.

The next victim was a widow with a two-year-old daughter, named Delphine Downing. Raymond was her lover within weeks of Janet's murder. Martha, again, became infuriated. They moved into the young woman's home in Michigan, as "brother and sister." Over time, they robbed her of her money and her possessions, then finally they forced sleeping pills down her throat. When she was unconscious, they shot her through the head. Beck drowned the crying child in a bathtub. The bodies were methodically buried in the cellar — a new covering of cement was poured over the gravesites — but suspicious neighbors had already reported Delphine's and Rainelle's disappearance.

Martha had grown close to the toddler, and when police came to the house, she seemed almost ready to let them in — not only into the home but into their macabre life, as well. The newly laid cement was discovered within the hour, and Martha and Raymond were taken into custody, in Michigan. They were extradited to New York to face the death penalty.

Both confessed to murdering Janet, and the mother and daughter, but when it came to the seventeen other related deaths, they were practically indignant. Other alleged victims included Raymond's first wife, who died in a "train accident" that never occurred. And another woman, Raymond claimed, died accidentally during a sexual interlude. "Exhaustion," he claimed.

During her trial, Martha Beck regularly dispatched letters from jail to the media about her and Raymond's sexual exploits, and their undying love. Theirs became a celebrity event. Raymond's sanity will always be questioned, but in spite of an insanity plea he was executed alongside Martha, on March 8, 1951, at Sing Sing Prison in New York State. This is one of the few cases of team-killers who never turned on each other in a final act of narcissism.

Finally, they claimed, they "had eternal love."

## KARLA HOMOLKA AND PAUL BERNARDO

In 1990, a young and good-looking Canadian, Karla Homolka, couldn't have been happier. She was engaged to marry a handsome, brilliant guy, Paul. Not only was he perfect to look at, and to listen to, he was also an accountant with a promising career. Karla loved Paul. She would do anything for him.

Paul did have a tendency to ask Karla to compromise herself. Sometimes she found herself engaging in sexual acts with other women while Paul watched, so that he could play out his fantasy of "having a virgin." He would order Karla to perform pornographic acts with whatever young girl they could lure in. He enjoyed video-taping the scenes, and then he would step in and penetrate the girl. Sometimes, Paul and Karla would have to drug a victim to sleep — whatever it took — Paul needed virgins at any cost.

In the beginning, Karla hadn't known about Paul's obsession with deflowering young women. Not yet 21 herself, she had thought she would be enough to satisfy him. But as the weeks and months passed, he let his disappointment be known that she hadn't been a virgin. Karla wanted Paul to be happy. It seemed that if she could go along with his suggestion and allow him this one desire he would be satiated; the virgin vessels ensured Paul's longevity in the relation-ship. Karla learned quickly — Paul would abandon her if he wasn't pleased. There was something both frightening and thrilling about a man who was so demanding.

On December 23, 1990, Miss Homolka and her fiancé would do something that sealed their relationship with horrific secrecy: they committed murder. Paul's desire to have his virgin had shifted slightly; the issue of virginity was becoming a "family problem." If Karla had disappointed him in this way, then she owed him her sis-ter. That, he explained, would be like having Karla for the first time. Through blood, through family, he could have a virgin and it would be a way of vicariously having Karla.

Karla brought home some halothane, an anesthetic, from her workplace at a veterinarian clinic. Mimicking what the doctors did with the animals, she planned to gently hold a rag full of the chemi-cal over her sister's face, after she'd fallen asleep. And then Paul could do anything he wanted.

Paul used his camcorder that night to take videos of the whole family — Mr. and Mrs. Homolka, their daughters Karla, Tammy and Lori, and the Christmas decorations that filled the home. Between filming and feigning the role of the perfect fiancé, Paul plied Tammy with Halcion-laced drinks. The effects were swift, and Tammy was passed out on the couch in minutes. When the other members of the household went upstairs to bed, Karla and Paul started to "work" on Tammy. Paul trained his lens on Tammy while he raped her, leaving Karla to keep the halothane-laden rag over her sister's face. Then he ordered Karla to make sexual advances on her sister.

At some point, Tammy threw up. Karla did what the doctors did at the clinic in such cases: she held her sister upside down and tried to clear her throat. Still, Tammy choked to death. Feeble at-tempts to revive her failed, so they dressed her, hid their drugs and camera, and called an ambulance. Karla's parents heard the vehicle drive up to the house. Everybody believed Tammy's death had been "accidental."

The couple had gotten away with murder. Karla may have been in shock, or perhaps she did not have it in her to grieve. Many people believe she moved on quickly so as not to lose step with Paul. He himself seemed matter-of-fact about the incident. He was irritated that Tammy had died, but was unemotional about the event. But then, Paul had been masking feelings for a lifetime.

Paul Bernardo did not grow up in a "normal" middle-class family like his girlfriend's. His old world-Italian father would beat his wife, an English woman, at the slightest cause. Life was full of contradictions: Kenneth was a financial success, having made good money in the tile business, but at home he was miserable. It was hard for Paul and his sister and brother to watch the many beatings. At some point, the children went their own ways; desperate to survive, they each found refuge outside the home. Paul had no sense of family. Paul's mother Marilyn ended up in the arms of her true love, a man her parents had rejected. It was from this relationship that Paul had been conceived. His father found out about the infidelity. He still gave Paul his last name, on his birth certificate, in 1964, but something changed after Paul's birth. His "father" now felt entirely free to do whatever he desired; after all, his wife was a whore.

Kenneth Bernardo began hanging around the neighborhood at night, peeping into windows, trying to get a glance at young girls. He fondled one child and ended up in court. Worst of all, he sexually abused his own daughter. His wife, Marilyn, became depressed and grotesquely obese. Rather than intervene and help her children, she withdrew. Housework came to a stop — weeks went by without cleaning, and rarely was there food in the refrigerator. And while neighbors and old friends note that Paul's siblings showed clear effects of abuse, Paul himself did not. Impeccably groomed each day, the handsome young cherub never left the house without his smile. One mother described him as "a perfect child. Polite, well-mannered, so sweet in his Boy Scout uniform. . ."

Paul had become involved in the Boy Scouts, and he worked summers as a counselor. He was the most popular leader at camp. He loved the Scouts, and shared his enthusiasm. At this point, in early adolescence, Paul did not even seem to notice girls — much less brood over deviant thoughts. The few dates he had were unre-markable. At worse, he was described as "a pleasant boy to spend time with." Paul was intelligent; he worked hard in school and held a series of responsible after-school jobs. He had a good head for fig-ures and showed the makings of a strong future in business. By fo-cusing on himself, rather than home, he was surviving. But then, something so pivotal would happen that even Paul would find he was not untouchable.

After a particularly harried argument with him, his mother Marilyn ran to dig out photos of his real father. At age 16, Paul learned the truth: he was a bastard. He was devastated. He became openly disrespectful to his mother, figuring that his father had seen something in her something that he had missed, that perhaps the abuse had been less inappropriate than he'd thought. He referred to her after that day only as "whore" or "slob." Between his mother's infidelity and his father's embarrassing perversions, he began to feel hate festering within him.

Paul's circle of friends began to change. He dropped out of sports and Scouting, he quit working after school. He hung out with petty thieves and druggies. His attitude in general and towards women in particular changed dramatically for the worse — and he enjoyed his newfound machismo.

In the early 1980s, Paul and his friend were recruited into the Amway business. Paul was once drawn in once more, as he had been with the Scouts. He used the techniques in his personal life, becoming the greatest salesman on earth. He didn't care as much about the product as the lessons he received on how to sell. He was working on himself. When he cruised the bars with his dubious friends, at night, he would practice new personas, different identities. With his good looks and charisma, he usually was successful in the art of seduction. He enjoyed his power over women. By the time Paul left for the University of Toronto, his fantasies had developed a darker side: he preferred anal sex, and demanded it from his sex mates. His temper had become volatile, and he had no qualms over beating a girlfriend who "acted up," whether at home or in public. Humiliation was another aphrodisiac.

To finance his schooling, Paul and a friend, Van Smirnis, started trafficking in stolen goods. Paul's appetite for toys, clothes and money could not be supported by a regular job. After graduation, he seemed to find legitimacy in his new career as a junior accountant at Price Waterhouse. Then, in October of 1987, he met Karla Homolka, and his world felt complete.

The two felt an immediate sexual attraction. And Karla told Paul she enjoyed his sadistic behaviors. A fantasy come true. One day, while he had her handcuffed, playing out a "victim role," and he asked her what she would think if it turned out this was more than a game: that he really was a rapist. She replied coolly, "perfect." His love deepened, and his rapes began.          ·

He had a pattern: he'd wait for a girl to get off a late evening bus, grab her from behind and pull her to the ground. After forcing anal sex and fellatio on her, talking all the while, he'd let her go. By 1988, thirteen women had been raped. Investigators referred to the assailant as the Scarsborough Rapist. Karla knew what Paul was doing, and encouraged him. It kept him happy — and as long as he was content, he never thought about leaving her.

Karla's greatest fear was the thought of Paul leaving. While Paul enjoyed his late night romps, he was becoming frustrated. He missed having Tammy around, so that he could play out his virgin fantasy. Karla immediately went to work: she recruited her friend, Jane — a 13-year-old who worked part-time at the clinic and idolized the older, pretty woman. She accepted an invitation to the Bernardos' new home, at 57 Bayview. Karla got Jane drunk on sweet alcoholic beverages (laced with Halcion). Then she called her fiancé to say that she had a surprise for him. He was in ecstasy when he came home to the virgin child, passed out on the couch. He wanted to know if this time, Karla knew what she was doing with the drugs. She assured him everything was under control, and so the couple went to work on the lifeless body. Jane never woke up, not even during a taped, brutal anal invasion. After the rape, Karla put Jane to bed. When she woke the next morning, she was curiously sore, but happy to "meet" Paul.

Paul was amazed at Karla's willingness to please him, and at the same time increasingly expected her to do more of the same. He toyed with her, to get more women. He told her at one point that she was too old to marry. She became distraught, and suicidal; and the wedding date was set. For Paul, it was economics: he put on a lavish event, keeping in mind that if he spent fifty dollars per plate, he'd end up with a hundred dollars in gifts or money per person. He anticipated a $50,000 return. He was right. But all the money, and the beautiful and obedient wife, were not enough. Inside, Paul's desires to possess women (or girls) was growing. Karla's attempts to satisfy his urge only fanned the flames.

Leslie Mahaffy, a truant who'd been locked out by her parents after once again coming home in the middle of the night, met up with Paul by pure coincidence on Friday, June 14, 1991. Paul was out augmenting his income by smuggling cigarettes across the U.S.-Canadian border, and had stopped to "borrow" some license plates off another car. He pulled a knife on Leslie and forced her into his car. While Karla slept, he began videotaping the nude, blindfolded

14-year-old. Karla awoke to hear muffled cries. Her only reaction was to question why Paul was using their good champagne glasses in her absence. Paul demanded that Karla make love to Leslie, disregarding her comments. He became the voice of a director in a film: every moment had to be perfect. After the prelude with Karla, Paul went in for the rough stuff. Karla held the camera.

On June 29, 1991, a couple out canoeing on Lake Gibson came across what appeared to be bits of animal flesh, splashed against cement blocks. On closer observation, it became obvious that this had been a person. The police were called. Leslie Mahaffy was identified by her teeth. Her body had been dismembered and thrown into shallow waters.

Meanwhile, young Jane, who was meant to satisfy Paul in between his episodes with his new type of victim, became unavailable. Jane's mother had become privy to what had become an open sexual relationship and she had disallowed further contact. It became difficult for Jane and Paul to meet. Paul was annoyed and Karla, typically, was scared.

On November 30, 1991, pretty and popular 14-year-old Terri Anderson was leaving her church parking lot. Karla, parked with her husband, beckoned her for directions. While the young girl talked with Karla, Paul pulled her into the backseat. She was drugged and raped, then murdered.

Following the same *modus operandi* on April 16, 1992, they lured Kristen French into their car. A horrific tape provided in court documents explicitly tells of her account:

> "I'm going to piss on you, okay? Then I'm going to shit on you. Don't make me mad. Don't make me hurt you. I won't piss in your face. You're a fucking piece of shit. But I like you. You look good covered in piss."

On April 30, Kristen's body was found in a ditch. She had not been dismembered, so officials thought the crimes were unrelated. On May 23, 1992, another body was found: it was Terri Anderson, lured months before from her church. The coroner told her father the death was a result of drugs — liquor and acid. In shock, Mr. Anderson couldn't understand how his daughter, a cheerleader and honor roll student, could possibly have drugged herself and then walked of her own accord into the brutal waters of Lake Ontario during a November freeze.

While investigators were making little headway with these cases, enough rape victims had come forward to provide a composite drawing. Red tape had kept the picture behind police doors for two years, but upon public release, Paul's previous colleagues at the accounting firm flooded the authorities with calls. Paul had quit his day job in favor of smuggling full-time.

The couple had moved to St. Catharines, Ontario, in the Niagara Falls area where the murder victims had been found. A base of operation was set up outside the area. Meanwhile, hours away, police were beginning to wonder about Paul Bernardo. Finally, he was tracked down and asked to provide semen samples. Test results proved that only 12% of the nation secreted the same semen type, so that Paul became a prime suspect in the rapes.

Bernardo remained cool on the surface, but behind closed doors he was no longer just irritable, he was aggressive and abusive. Strangely enough, even Karla had her limits: she would not accept being hit. And so she called the police. It was January, 1993.

During a routine interview with the Niagara Police, Karla grew paranoid. The rape investigation was intensifying. To distance herself from Paul, she turned on him. Her tragic tale of captivity at the hands of a madman made front-page news. Paul Bernardo was arrested. Trial dates were set, and deals were cut: Karla would give up information on the murders in exchange for immunity. The government agreed.

In early March, Karla was checked into a psychiatric hospital. During this time, she wrote a confessional letter to her parents, telling the truth behind Tammy's death. Surprisingly, they have maintained a semblance of a family relationship. Doctors at the hospital were on her side, saying that "(Karla) knew what was happening but felt helpless and unable to act in her own defense or in anyone else's defense. She was paralyzed with fear and in that state, became obedient and self-serving."

Paul's trial was deferred for two years. Prosecutors got hold of the videotapes, and that was a step that Paul's first attorney, Ken Murray, was unprepared to handle. He quit. After some postponement, veteran defense lawyer John Rosen took his place.

In May of 1995, Bernardo's trial finally began. Judge Patrick LeSage listened, along with the jury and courtroom, to the devastating tapes and watched the shocking videos. The beginning of the trial may have been delayed, but the conviction was quick: On September 1, 1995 Paul Bernardo was convicted on all the charges against him: the kidnappings, rapes and murders of Leslie Mahaffy and Kristen French. He also faced trials in the death of Tammy Homolka and the serial rapes in Scarborough. Under Canadian law, he can apply for parole after 25 years in prison, thought it is unlikely he would be successful in his bid.

Karla ended up with two 12-year sentences, with a minimum of three years to be served. Many believe she was as titillated by the events as Paul was. Some people hold that she was another victim. Depending on your view, she was either convicted properly for her part in Paul's deviant escapades, or she managed the greatest bargain in Canadian history, by cleverly manipulating her cooperation with the government to engineer one of the most generous deals that Canada has ever made with a criminal witness. Time will tell.

Even when the team is all-female, there is one dominant member who orchestrates the activities and at least one submissive, easily-manipulated partner. Usually they are in a sexual relationship, which for at least one of the partners is "enhanced" by the murders. Actually, female killers exhibit a wider variety of rationales than most others. Some do it to increase sexual stimulation; but some just do it for the money they can take. Some like the attention and excitement that swirls around after a dramatic event, and get a kick out of seeing what they can get away with.

One difference between all-women teams and male/female teams is that male predators usually look for sexually-attractive female victims, while women teams often target frail, incapacitated, elderly persons, or infants — in other words, victims who are easily controlled and easily killed.

All-female teams may also fit the "Angels of Death" model. Here, women's presumed roles as caretaker can be exaggerated to the point of inversion. Some take actions that are likely to cause the death of a target, but then call attention to the mysterious emergency and bring about a last-minute rescue, thereby winning praise all around. Of course, if the rescue part doesn't work, they can always try again on someone else. In other cases, the killer(s) may kindly put suffering people "out of their misery," as an act of "mercy." That involves a unilateral decision, of course, as to what constitutes mercy.

Their range of victims may be greater, and their reasons for killing may be different, but in the end, as with all teams, it is usually a "falling out" between the partners that provides police the opening they need in order to identify and convict these killers.

Gwendolyn Graham, during my study, wrote me a letter, simply saying:

> *A few items around our old house that belonged to persons who were killed did not conjure my sentence, cannot bring about a sentence alone. I was the victim of my ex lover's obsession with me. I feel Catherine was out to cross me; the only so-called evidence comes in the form of gossip from my co-workers, probably biased because we were gay, considered evil on that alone. When I left for Texas, no one could find a hint of violence... if anyone did commit the murders, it would be the unstable woman from my past. I didn't know. I just left her because of her instability. I would have tried to help. Now, ironically, I am alone to rot because of her, and no one can do a thing to help that...*
>
> *Gwen*

Gwendolyn Graham and Catherine Wood were 24 and 23 years old, working as nurses, and actively committing murders in 1987. While Gwendolyn's letter tells a different story, they were convicted of murder in connection with a sexual thrill that they enjoyed while suffocating patients at the Alpine Manor nursing home, in Walker, Michigan. Catherine Wood was the main witness for the prosecution. Here's how the story goes, according to her — and according to the jury, which accepted her version during the their trials in 1989.

Graham and Wood were lesbians, in love. Talking about fantasies, in October of 1986, Gwendolyn admitted that thinking about murder heightened her sexuality. Their intimate relationship had already included bondage, choking and other rough play; but Gwendolyn seemed to have a penchant for the "real thing."

At first, according to Wood, she didn't take Graham seriously. Catherine considered these fantasies some sort of macabre joke; but in January of 1987, Gwendolyn murdered a woman. She'd decided to kill six persons; and their initials would spell "murder." But the scheme proved too complicated. Some of the potential victims were too young, too hard to kill. She would have to settle for women whose names didn't add up to "murder," but were at least more frail.

The woman was thought to have died from natural causes; her body was found lifeless, in bed. Gwendolyn told Catherine that she had murdered her; and instead of turning her in to the authorities, Catherine joined her the next time around. So, between January and April, the team killers attacked at least a dozen patients and successfully killed five.

They were organized, and the tactic was always the same: Catherine served as lookout while Gwendolyn would move into a room, take a damp cloth, and press it over the victim's mouth and nose. After the murder was done, she would take her lover into a vacant room at Alpine Manor and indulge in perverse sexual activities, titillated by the thrilling recollection of the murder. The victims ranged in age from 60 to 95 years, and mostly were suffering from Alzheimer's: Marguerite Chambers, 60; Edith Cole, 89; Mirckle Luce, 95; Mae Lacen, 79; and Belle Burkhart, 74.

The team was methodical in their actions, careful, never leaving evidence behind — and certainly, never a witness. But in mid-April, Gwendolyn Graham made a huge mistake — she took another lover. Catherine Wood's lack of inclination to participate physically in the killings had frustrated Graham, and she'd begun to lose interest in her and their "team efforts." Sex, even after murder, lost its thrill; Wood's lack of desire to kill dampened Graham's fervor.

According to Wood, Graham decided to leave her lover and her job at Alpine (with all the ripe potential victims waiting there), to begin a new life. She followed her latest lover to Texas, where she took a job as a nurse's aide at St. Francis Hospital.

Wood was despondent, abandoned, and alone to consider her actions. . . she was plagued with guilt. Very little conversation took place between the ex-lovers and murderers after Graham moved. She'd acclimated easily to her new life, at the new hospital, with her new lover. Wood begged her to think again and come back to her; Graham laughed.

Wood was devastated; she began to lose her grip. Co-workers recall remarking that she seemed fragile, shaky, and would cry easily. She could no longer bear her guilt. She told her ex-husband about the killings and her part in all of it, admitting for the first time that she had had a sexual relationship with Graham. She told her ex-husband that she was confessing because Gwendolyn had mentioned (during a couple of their sporadic phone calls) that, working in the infant ward, she'd begun to feel an urge to "smash a child's head." Wood thought it was time for the killing to stop.

Kenneth Wood didn't know whether to believe his former

wife. In his opinion, she was probably half-psychotic over the break-up, and this manic behavior and outlandish story would only be part of that. Probably, she was suffering from depression. Still, over the year, Catherine stood by her story. Her emotional condition improved. Kenneth no longer believed she was speaking only as a vindictive scorned lover — he believed her, now, and so he went to local authorities in the fall of 1988.

The police checked out the story and found that it was conceivable that at least eight of the recent deaths at Alpine Manor might not have been due to "natural causes." Another five were definite murders. By December, warrants were out, and both women were arrested.

Gwendolyn was at work and was taken quite by surprise when the police walked in. Her bail was set at one million dollars. An investigation was instigated immediately to determine whether Graham had continued her murderous spree, but apparently she had not. There had been no suspicious deaths since her arrival at the hospital.

At a hearing to determine whether the lovers should be tried for murder, the prosecution relied heavily on Catherine Wood's conversations with her husband and on co-workers who claimed to have overheard incriminating conversations between the lovers, plus souvenirs found at the couples' old home.

Several co-workers remembered the souvenirs brought out during trial — and knew who had been their previous owners. This was only circumstantial evidence, but it proved helpful. Prosecutors were able to bind the women for first-degree murder, leading them toward a trial. On the 8th of September, just days before her trial, Wood pled guilty in the Alpine Manor murders and agreed to testify against Graham, in return for protection. Gwen's case took an unexpected turn for the worse. After five hours of deliberation, the jury found her guilty on five counts of murder and one count of conspiracy to commit murder.

Wood broke down during testimony, explaining that "[she] said she wanted to smash babies. I had to stop her."

On October 11, 1989, Wood appeared in front of circuit judge Robert Benson at Kent County, and received a sentence of twenty-to-forty years. The judge noted that the deaths never would have been solved without her help, that she showed remorse, and that she definitely had been the follower, not the leader.

On December 2, 1989, Gwendolyn Graham received six life terms in prison, without possibility of parole. She continues to deny her role in the killings, blaming her fate simply on her lover's insanity.

Some women come together for the purpose of killing for profit. They may not be involved in a sexual relationship, but they always fall into the roles of a dominant figurehead and a willing partner.

Such was the case of Amelia Sach and Annie Waters, over 100 years ago.

Amelia Sach was born in 1873 in England. Annie Waters was born in 1869, also in England. This was the first documented team to operate in the 20th century. Just after 1900, Amelia and Annie, friends and neighbors living in a small community, decided to go into business together: baby farming. Under the guise of an adoption service, they solicited themselves as nurturing women, offering housing for unwed mothers, feeding and helping pregnant women and young mothers until their babies could be properly placed in good families.

Few questions were asked; the pregnant women's parents were simply relieved to find a place where they could send their daughters, to maintain their anonymity until the infants were adopted. One of the attractive aspects of this particular residence was that the operators kept no records; therefore, everyone could have complete confidence that children would not come back to tarnish their mother's reputations at some later date. Sadly, the lack of records would later obscure how many children had actually been murdered.

Amelia Sach was the dominant figure in the relationship, and in the killings. In fact, Annie Waters was diagnosed as "feeble," which, in modern terms, probably translates best as "mentally inca-pacitated." She could no more carry out a killing operation than run a business. She could only follow simple, very direct orders — and she held no capacity to understand the nature of her actions. She was the perfect partner for the greedy Amelia.

Sach took complete control over all areas of the business. She advertised their services in confidential, local rag sheets in the Lon-don area where they had taken up residence. Sach was as shocked as anyone when she discovered the enormous demand for their ser-vices. There was a constant stream of clients — babies were born, and she found herself having to care for them while impatiently waiting for families to come along. Selling the infants had proven profitable, but the enforced waiting periods took away from her in-come. Mothers were allowed to stay on until the babies had been farmed out, and the infants needed clothing and food.

Sach became anxious. She was unwilling to bear the cost of providing for the children or their mothers. She devised a scheme, beginning with rather more efforts to preserve the confidentiality. She explained to the mothers that children waited longer to be places when the adoptive parents' identities had to be revealed. If the mothers were willing to allow the process to go forward with-out knowing the new parents' identities, more babies would be sold — and faster. Most of the women, under their rather desperate circumstances, then waived their right to know their child's new home. They found their proprietor to be correct: the babies disappeared much more quickly, and the mothers went back to their lives. What no one knew was that the infants were no longer being adopted, they were being murdered.

Annie Walters took orders from her boss without question. Amelia would hand a baby over to her, and tell her that the child had to be killed. She had worked out an easy method. Annie would simply poison the victims, using chlorodine; then she would take their little corpses to one of the near-by junkyards or sometimes to the Thames River, and dump them. Amelia would provide the mothers with a terse explanation — a vague story assuring them that their babies were in "good hands" — and proceed to ask for an additional "processing fee." The relieved parent and her family readily paid.

Eventually, Sach made a suspicious move: she took a baby home to the flat they shared. She planned to have Annie meet her and poison the infant there, then dispose of it. As coincidence would have it, their landlord happened to also work as a London police officer. He noticed the baby with the women one day, and its disappearance the next. He found that odd, but considering that they ran an adoption agency, he gave it little thought. The following week, they brought home another child and, again, it disappeared as quickly as it had arrived. This time the officer called his on his colleagues, and asked the authorities to take a look at the lodging facility.

Chlorodine was found and after some digging, literally, so were some tiny corpses. Amelia Sach and Annie Walters were immediately arrested. All the way to the gallows, Sach protested. Waters was more compliant. Mr. Pierrepoint, the hangman, had this to say about them. "These two women were baby-farmers of the worst kind and were both repulsive in type." Apparently, there was little sympathy for Annie's feeble-mindedness.

The women were hanged in 1903. Neither one provided any clues regarding the missing children. Without any records to go by, investigators were never able to come up with an accurate count. It has been conjectured that at least two dozen children were murdered, given how long the women were operating, the number of mothers and children who lodged at the residence, and the unconscionable actions of Amelia Sach — her desire for profit at any cost.

The only way to tell that a nurse is killing patients is when the mortality rate goes up so much at her work place that it tips off suspicions. In most hospitals, those targeted by killer-caretakers are the most frail, the most elderly or the terminally ill. Thus, the perpetrator may go unrecognized for a long, long time— the deaths were expected anyway.

In recent years, deaths in hospitals have been given closer study; the findings show that, in spite of the Hippocratic Oath, there appears to be a fraction of doctors and nurses who seek out their professions in order to gain easy access to defenseless victims. Hospital administrators sometimes stand in the way of investigation, even when there is ample reason for suspicion. Often, the killing caretaker(s) have good reputations and administration is reluctant to entertain dramatic allegations, when death is a daily occurrence in such institutional environments.

Of course, as awareness of the issue rises, investigations are now conducted somewhat more readily when suspicions are aroused. Regulations are changing, and even if the administration at a given hospital or nursing home is desensitized to death and unwilling to take a fresh look at its staff, investigations are sometimes leading to the apprehension of healthcare professionals who used to be able to work with impunity. Still, there are cases in which all efforts to investigate, and full cooperation on the part of the hospital, are in vain. Nurses (and doctors) still get away with murder.

In Ann Arbor, Michigan, in 1975, there was an inexplicable increase in mortality at the Veteran's Administration Hospital between July and August. The cause of death was the same in every case: respiratory arrest requiring dramatic intervention on the part of care providers. In this case, the number was so alarming that the administrators initiated the investigation. At least 30 patients suffered these respiratory bouts, some several times over, and in total 9 patients died. Another 11 to 25 are suspected of having been murdered, as well, but their cases are still unresolved.

Administrators were certain they were dealing with a so-called "Angel of Death" scenario. That is, a woman (or women) — very rarely men, seeking attention by saving lives and the adulation they received from colleagues for their heroic achievements.

Autopsies and probes into the survivors proved that at least 18 of the victims had been injected with a lethal dose of the muscle relaxant Pavulon, a synthetic form of the lethal poison curare. Pavulon, when used properly, works as a painkiller; but it is deadly if the patient is overdosed.

Federal investigators were brought in to help the administration. Their first objective was to single out the ward or the shift — or both — when most of the respiratory arrests were occurring. They learned that most of the drama occurred during the late afternoon shift, in the Intensive Care Unit. Authorities then had to find out how the drug was being administered to the patients. An examination of the treatment records for each patient in that ward,

during that shift, showed that Pavulon had been administered intra-
venously through feeding tubes. It was rather brilliant on the part of
the killer(s): the procedure is so routine that it would not require
supervision by higher professionals, would not raise suspicions
among patients and their families, and was not monitored, generally
speaking, by hospital staff.

Investigators now knew how, what, when and where. The
next step was to find out "who". They reviewed a list of nurses.
They compared the staff's work routines with the attack times and
locations. It didn't take long to find that 29-year-old Filipina Narciso and 31-year-old Leonora Perez were the two nurses in atten-
dance with all victims in question.

Next, survivors were questioned about their relationships with
the nurses. One elderly woman explained that, after she complained
about her feeding tube, Leonora Perez had nodded but then turned
and walked out of her room, leaving the tube in place. Another patient, a 60-year-old man, told authorities that Perez had come into
his room to take care of him, finding him unexpectedly screaming in
the midst of a respiratory arrest. Instead of helping him, she had
fled.

The two women were arrested and faced multiple charges of
murder. Both adamantly denied any wrongdoing, but in July of 1977,
the women went to trial and were found guilty on all counts. Not
six months later, a charge of insufficient evidence was brought
against the prosecutors. Claims that the trial was based on errone-
ous information and legal errors resulted in the release of both Perez
and Narciso.

The whole episode thus remains inconclusive. And while no
one is certain what became of the women (they may well be at work
in another hospital today), one thing is certain: the deaths at the
Veterans' Administration Hospital stopped once the two were relieved of their duties.

# PART III
## MALE/MALE TEAM KILLERS

Not always homosexual, but always exhibiting a dominator/ dominated structure, this form of "male bonding" goes far beyond the normal male-buddy relationship. Even when males team together as heterosexuals, and without any apparent sexual component based on their own "union," there are aspects of the relationship that render it unusual. For example, Kenneth Bianchi (*aka* the Hillside Strangler) achieved climax when killing along with his cousin, Angelo Buono. Under police suspicion, he moved away from their "killing ground" in Los Angeles to the state of Washington. But Kenneth found that, without Angelo, killing just wasn't the same.

Homosexual killing teams reflect much the same characteristics as their heterosexual counterparts, and they also have much in common with female/female killing teams. However, statistically, male homosexuals are far more sadistic in their killing rituals than females. The case of Dean Corll and Wayne Henley makes this point.

Ultimately, most homosexual teams break down over fidelity within the unit, something that is threatened each time a victim is chosen. The weaker partner becomes increasingly upset, while the dominant team member usually claims that having sex with the victims "doesn't count" as infidelity. He justifies it as a shared relationship, insofar as both members of the team are aware of the victim and engage in sexual activity/torture. Predictably, the dominant male will need to reach out to other men, on his own. He will seek a new partner, a lover. . . someone less a victim and more his equal. A potential new team member. Then "love" between the partners is replaced with hatred and vengeance, bitterness and accusations. In most cases, fear of losing her or his lover — if not fear of being killed — is what forces the more passive team killer to turn on the leader, sometimes reporting him to the authorities.

## DEAN CORLL AND WAYNE HENLEY

Friends and neighbors affectionately called Dean Allen Corll the "Candyman." Not only had he run a candy store (with a partner), he was extremely generous with his goodies, providing children with his sweets, which earned him friendship and trust — his calculated goal.

Inside his home, Corll became something of a magician — children disappeared after a visit to his quaint, tidy residence. Concerned that his good name might fall under suspicion, Dean enlisted the aid of Wayne Elmer Henley, an adolescent boy whom he paid in drugs and money in exchange for providing him less-identifiable children — always boys.

Like Dean's persona, his home, too, masked a darker, deeper secret: as cunning as the Candyman was at procuring victims, so was he accomplished at creating a chamber of horrors where he could play with them. In various hidden spaces throughout his lair, he had devised meticulous torture tools and fixtures, all hidden from the unsuspecting eye.

And while Dean was mostly recognized for his assortment of treats, he was also known, among a certain segment, for his drugs. For older boys who paid him a visit, he was prepared to offer glue, cocaine and alcohol. Of course, all drugs came at the price of having sex.

Henley was impressed with Corll — in his 30s, and more than twice the boys' age, Dean appeared controlled, and financially stable. This was much more than he was offered in his own home. Wayne came from a broken family and seemed confused by Dean Corll's role in his life: Dean was demanding, but offered a certain sense of security; and when he was with him, as he explains, "*I felt I had a home, a sense of family — as twisted as it all ended up being.*" [1] When Dean wasn't busy preying on children, he and Wayne carried on sexually.

Dean proudly displayed the latest attribute to his chamber, a plank of wood he dubbed the torture board, and asked Wayne to help him handcuff his drugged victims to it. Wayne was then to watch, while the Candyman proceeded to sodomize and torture children. Wayne was asked, on many occasions, to participate.

The sessions with unidentified vagrants and hitchhikers included torture. "*We pulled out pubic hairs, one at a time, and shoved glass rods up the penis or shoved large, bullet-like instruments in the rectums.*" Wayne made this grisly disclosure during his 1974 testimony. [2]

Even twenty years after the event, experts still disagree about the relationship between Dean Corll and Wayne Henley. All that is certain is that Wayne, on one hand, had fallen into a dependent relationship with a seeming stable man. But on the other hand, once the "real" Dean revealed his killing side, Wayne was too terrified to do anything but comply; not only continuing the relationship, but aiding in the killings and in disposing of the many bodies.

[1] *The Man With the Candy*, Jack Olsen, p. 387
[2] Wayne Henley, Copies, Transcript *Corll/Henley vs. Texas*, October, 1974

Drugs seemed to calm Dean, helping him maintain his control over their murderous lifestyle. Conversely, Wayne exhibited signs of a growing paranoia; psychologists diagnose a drug-induced psychosis. The killers had murdered so many boys that they'd been forced to rent a space for disposal. At night, the victims were driven to the shed Corll had leased, and buried beneath it.

Between the drugs, the body count and the revolting work of relocating and hiding dead bodies, Wayne was exhausted; he'd had enough. He went to a friend, David Owen Brooks, who had initially introduced him to Corll, and sought his help. David had been privy to some of the torture/murder sessions himself, but had managed to fall out of the bigger picture. He agreed to go with Wayne to Dean's house, and try and "talk sense" to him.

Dean, confronted, was infuriated. Wayne, in turn was more frightened than ever. The next morning he returned with two of his buddies, a teenaged boy and his girlfriend. He hoped to make peace over a glue-sniffing session.

August 8, 1973 found Dean more volatile than the day before. After feigning a truce, and after the three kids had passed out from the glue, the nightmare began. Dean dragged Wayne to the torture board and cuffed him, high, so that his body was dangling. More than anything else, Dean was enraged that a female had been admitted into his home; this was his homosexual fantasyland, and women were not welcome. Wayne would be murdered for two days of betrayal.

Wayne came to, enough to try to appease his sometime lover and co-murderer; he begged for Dean's forgiveness. He promised he would "do" the girl — torture and rape her — if Dean would just spare him. Knowing how to appeal to Dean, Wayne added that Dean should be in charge of "teaching the boy a lesson."

Dean let Wayne go, replacing his body with the drugged, hardly-conscious visitors. Tired of placating Corll, Henley grabbed the Candyman's gun and fired six times, leaving his master face down in a pool of his own blood. He then called the Pasadena Police Department and calmly stated that he'd killed a man. It was 8:30 AM. By 8:45, officers had arrived at the house on Lanar Street in Pasadena, Texas. Taking the victims down from their torture board, the police realized that they were so drugged they had no idea what had happened — that someone had been killed, and that it was they who were the intended victims.

Wayne Henley was taken into custody. Within days, David Owen Brooks joined him, charged with conspiracy to murder. Wayne was eager to give up the locations of the shed and the other burial sites he was familiar with. Just six inches below the surface, the police struck the first of 17 bodies: a young boy wrapped in a plastic bag, a noose still tight around his neck.

The investigating team was led next to Lake Sam Rayburn, where Wayne showed them four more burial sites. At High Island, six more bodies were found. Including some that Dean Corll had hidden himself and have yet to be discovered, the body count is estimated to be 32.

Wayne Henley received little mercy for his too-late show of conscience: a "jury of his peers" gave him six terms of 99 years' imprisonment at a Texas State facility. And for his part, David Brooks received a life sentence for conspiracy to murder.

## LAWRENCE BITTAKER AND ROY NORRIS

When FBI profiler John Douglas was asked "who the most frightening man he'd profiled might be?", he responded without hesitation: Lawrence Bittaker.[1]

Roy Norris unwittingly described who the dominant figure in this killing team was when he stated to me that,

> "I only wanted to... have women. Laying around watching women on the beach. . . I could maintain my erection for hours. That felt better than the orgasm. They call it autosexual. I didn't enjoy killing. That was Lawrence. It was his favorite part — watching the women struggle to live, both knowing he would soon be taking life away. But the sex, I'm guilty of enjoying that. It's just, if not for him, my fear of him turning his wires and ice picks on me. . . I would not have participated. You don't have to believe me, everyone knows I was the one that 'fessed us. You asked me if I thought the guy would tell. My friend, the guy I told... He wasn't a murderer. I think I knew. But I saw no way out, alive except prison..."
>
> Letter from Pelican Bay, Maximum Facility, 1999

---

[1] *Hunting Humans*, p. 423

Roy Norris met Lawrence Bittaker as a cell-mate at the Men's Colony near San Luis Obispo, California in the late 1970s. Norris had been charged with sexually assaulting his girlfriend; although his explanation to me is that he ". . . *agreed to let her cry rape when we were caught in the middle of things, to save her reputation.*" He claims he chose a short stint in prison to let her get off easy. And while Roy Norris had experienced a rough childhood that may have played a role in his future acts of violence toward women — the result of an unwanted pregnancy, within a sullen marriage, and a childhood of abuse — it couldn't compare with Lawrence Bittaker's, or the rage that followed. Cast off to foster care by his single, drug-addicted mother, he explains that

> [His life] consisted of hopping from home to home watching checks come in, meant to pay for my food, but it was the family who ate. I was given the other kids' clothes, even the girls', and often, I spent time in Spanish-speaking families. No food, no clothes, no fucking talking. I hated Spics. Stole from me, you know? When I was no more than a kid. And no one believes a kid. When you tell about rape. It happens to men, too. I think I got tripped on sex, three-ways, violence because I had that. And no one, no agency jumped to jail those bastards. You grow up and it's normal sex — like anything else wouldn't feel right, or get me off.

Prison terms brought together two men, who shared histories of dysfunctional relationships and damaged sexual tendencies. Bittaker's desire, upon release, to grab some "chicks" seemed fine to Norris They'd finally have their way. That would be a change.

As planned, their meeting place was a hotel in Los Angeles. They pulled their money together and purchased a van they dubbed the "Murder Mac." And then, they began to cruise.

On June 24, 1979 they picked up sixteen-year-old Cindy Schaeffer. She was just another girl, enjoying the sun at Redondo

Beach, until the two men introduced her to a terror she never knew possible. *"I still see her face, everyday. It haunts me most,"* Norris offers. The duo bundled Cindy in a blanket and drove to the mountains and then, in a secluded area, proceeded to brutally raped and torture the girl. Just before they jointly strangling her with a wire coat hanger, she begged for "only a second, to pray." Norris related that detail to me in a letter.

Remorse was no deterrent. Dumping the body, they were soon back on the streets, scouting. Along the Pacific Coast Highway, Route 101, they picked up Andrea Hall on July 8. The abuse escalated: her sexual abuse and torture lasted almost two days. When Bittaker was finally "done" with the victim, he rammed an ice pick through her ear, into her brain.

In early September, the killers picked up two friends, lured by the prospect of a beer and some pot. Fifteen-year-old Jackie Gilliam and thirteen-year-old Leah Lamp were strangled and their dead bodies were tossed over a deep canyon side; both were naked and revealing signs of the killers' method of operation: rape, torture and murder.

According to Norris, Bittaker was out of control. *"He was packing a gun, making threats. Me, included. I just... kept my mouth shut. He was the boss."*

On Halloween their spree would come to an end, but not before one final murder. The team had stopped for coffee; Shirley Ledford was their unsuspecting waitress. Her two errors were being in the wrong place, and being Hispanic. That excited Bittaker. Violent fantasies aroused him. Here was his perfect victim. So perfect that Bittaker wanted to memorialize the session by recording it. Ms. Ledford was raped, and her elbow was crushed repeatedly with blows from Bittaker sledgehammer. After hours of pain and near-death suffering, Shirley Ledford screamed, "Do it! Just kill me!" And so they did. [2]

A few weeks later, Norris ran into another ex-convict from the Men's Colony. He shared his experiences of the past few months. As Norris says, *"The friend told jurors that the man was too terrified to stop [meaning me], to stand up to this dominant figure. I did horrible things, I did them in the face of my fear of dying: I let them, instead of me…"*

While the friend pitied Norris for his involvement in the story, his conscience forced him to talk. Both perpetrators were arrested and ultimately charged equally with five counts of murder, kidnapping and forcible rape, sexual perversion and criminal conspiracy.

Suddenly, behind bodyguards and with Bittaker in shackles, Roy Norris testified against his "leader" and was, in return, granted immunity from the death penalty. He received forty-five years to life with parole eligibility in 2010. He serves his sentence at Pelican Bay, Maximum Security, in California.

Lawrence Bittaker's trial ended with a sentence to die ordered on February 17, 1981, in twenty-six guilty verdicts — five for murder. He awaits execution at San Quentin, in California.

Roy Norris played the role of "victim" to his captor. In some ways he was. But a self-admitted "autosexual," he wrote his longest letter to me following the release of the movie *Kiss the Girls*, starring Morgan Freeman and Ashley Judd. The subject matter was sex slaves.

Roy provided a list of information he "needed," including exact dialogue from the movie, an explanation of how the victims were kidnapped and where they were held. How many victims, exactly? Did the captor keep them tied, or drugged? And as a footnote, he offered his disdain toward Ms. Judd: "She really let herself go — women who have the potential to be sexually attractive should live

---

[2] According to taped transcripts, Los Angeles Police Dept.

up to it." He condemned her for playing a rugged kick-boxer — signs of power, lack of femininity.

So what does this mean? While Roy Norris may not have been the "natural killing machine" his accomplice was, he certainly had no capacity to respect women. Further, he still relates to women as objects, provided solely to offer themselves as sexual stimuli, and not as human lives.

In these ways, he is as dangerous as his partner, who still claims the tape of their last session *"doesn't prove anything except a three-some... she's the one who got out of hand. She's the one who said 'kill me...'"* Bittaker denies the profundity of their crimes; Norris hides behind an autosexual tendency. Either way, they represent terror beyond comprehension.

Kenneth Bianchi's mother couldn't have been more supportive. When her son told her there was no scope for his talents in their hometown of Rochester, New York, she had to agree. A man with high ambitions, he saw Hollywood as a better launch pad.

Ken's favorite television show was "Chips," a program about the lives of two motorcycle cops who worked a district of Los Angeles, usually along the ocean. He figured he'd head down to southern California and take up a position not unlike the actors'. He thought little of the academic and physical tests or the years of training involved. But his mother said nothing — Mrs. Bianchi regarded the years she'd spent raising her adopted son from the age of two as grueling, at best. He'd suffered social problems at school, and bedwetting throughout most of his adolescence; and he was known to give way to fits of rage. Better to let him go and seek his fortune on the other side of the country.

At 26, he was newly divorced and ready to make a fresh start. No one could agree more than his mother. She picked up the phone, and relying on their Italian blood, called in a family favor. Though she didn't know Angelo Buono personally, he was from the same neighborhood and the same bloodline (although the tie was thin); he was a cousin to Kenneth Bianchi. Best of all, he owned an upholstery shop in Los Angeles, Ken's dreamland. So, in 1976, Ken packed up his belongings and left home, heading for Tinsel Town.

I wrote to Bianchi, years later, as part of my research. He explained in a letter to me that

> *"I had had both women — the good girls who had to be married or at least promised marriage to give it away, and the girls just born to give it away; I was good-looking, you know? I could have it either way. But the only job [available in Rochester] was like working at the big Kodak factory or some fucked job like that. I needed opportunity. I demanded that of myself."*

But living with Angelo didn't sound like opportunity, after all. In Ken's mind, being an upholstery shop owner sounded boring. But Angelo's life turned out to be nothing like the cover he used. When Ken got a glimpse of the life he really lived, he would stand in awe. Behind Angelo's shop, the man was keeping a private harem, and his vicious demeanor kept his sex slaves from daring to ask for money — or to leave.

Angelo Buono had a history of intimidating women. He had married several times and fathered at least six children, but not one of his ex-wives and girl friends asked for alimony or palimony. By his own sadistic standards, he had a grand life. Sex with young girls at a snap of his fingers, and sex as violent as he wanted it. His children respected him, surprisingly, and came around often; yet he never had to worry about their pestering mothers. His shop did well, financially. He worked hard, and over time became known as the upholsterer to the stars. Why would he want Ken around? If anything, he would be a hindrance. Still, he was family, and so it was only right to allow him to stay while he got on his feet.

When Ken arrived in Los Angeles, he was floored. The main boulevards had everything a man could want: prostitutes, drugs, pornography. . . from his small life in Rochester to this land of opportunity. And when he moved in with Angelo, the women were readily available to serve his needs. Angelo was proud of his achievements — and of his farm of women. But at some point Angelo's temper, and Ken's need for celebrity, both needed an outlet. One cousin was a walking time bomb, the other was more a naïve braggart dying to see his name in lights.

Angelo's rage would become murderous, and Ken's need to hang onto Angelo, to prove his loyalty and possibly see his name in the papers, would all become real when a prostitute "betrayed" the elder cousin.

Angelo had called an escort service and hired a prostitute for himself and Ken. They had both been brutal, beating and sodomizing the woman. She made the mistake of telling her pimp, who began to harass the men. Angelo set out to prove who the bigger man was. Unable, however, to find the pimp, he decided to send a message via an attack on another of his girls. Yolanda Washington, a well-known prostitute who worked for that pimp, always worked the same corner of Sunset Boulevard. Ken and Angelo focused on her. She was known for the vibrant colors and dangling jewelry she wore; it contrasted brilliantly against her dark skin. Around 11:00 PM, on Halloween in 1977, the two men paid Yolanda for her time. While a woman who is paid for sex expects to "perform," what happened to Yolanda was horrific, beyond anything within the realm of normalcy. Once they had her inside Angelo's car, Bianchi beat, sodomized and viciously penetrated the woman. Her pleas for help — which Kenneth later recalled during court testimony — went ignored. Angelo drove until it was his turn, when he took out on her his rage at being kicked while she was trying to fight off Ken in the backseat. Once both men had abused her sexually, Ken strangled her to death. They drove along the freeway until they came to a rea-sonable dumping ground, the Forest Lawn Cemetery. There, her body was later found, nude, spread-eagled in a significant setting — her vagina "pointing" toward the graveyard. The police figured, at first, that either a John or her pimp had done it. No one imagined this was part of a crime series.

Finally, Kenneth Bianchi and Angelo Buono had a something in common: they enjoyed sadism and destroying women. Tensions di-minished between the cousins, with their shared secret and new-found thrill. Ken created a pattern of falling out of one job and into the next, but Angelo, in spite of his own work ethic, easily disre-garded his younger cousins' irresponsible lifestyle. The pleasures of raping and killing clearly outweighed any personal conflict.

Judy Miller, 15 years old, was the team's next victim. She worked at a restaurant on the Boulevard, but had recently men-tioned toying with prostitution. The tips weren't very good, and the gals from the street would come in for coffee, bragging about the great money they made as hookers. Angelo found the girl, standing under a streetlamp, alone. He had let Ken off at a bus stop, and told him to walk around the corner where he'd meet up with him once he'd gotten his "target." After a conversation, Judy agreed to get in the car. Angelo picked up Ken and kept on driving. The men told Judy that she was under arrest. She protested, claiming she wasn't soliciting. Still, they would not allow her out of the car. She asked where they were headed and was told that they were taking her to a special crimes unit (Angelo's house). Kenneth handcuffed Judy. Once inside the house, Angelo coaxed the frightened girl, who now realized these were not cops; he whispered words like "baby," and "hush now... it'll be alright."

Then she was stripped, and raped in a back bedroom. The men flipped a coin to see who'd go first. Afterward, Angelo used his up-holstery materials — duct tape, rope and foam — to stuff her mouth and control her body. She could not stop shaking. Angelo's biggest concern was that she might wet his carpet. He strangled her with a noose and kept a plastic bag over her head as she sucked violently for her last breath. When it was over, Kenneth gathered her belongings and took the few dollars from her purse; then they bundled her into the trunk of the car. She was found at 2844 Alta Terrace Drive in La Crescenta. Angelo had recently been rejected by the girl who lived there, and hoped she'd discover the body.

Angelo and Kenneth were thrilled with their new game. In all my research, I have not come across a killing duo who enjoyed their murders so much. Kenneth combed the newspapers, looking for his name. It was all he could do not to brag. Angelo's biggest complaint was that Ken might blow things, if he didn't keep his mouth shut. At the same time, he was dreaming up a new plan. Hookers were easy. Angelo wanted to find a "real" woman.

Using fake police badges, Buono and Bianchi drove along a winding road in the Hollywood Hills, playing "Chips." They pulled over Lissa Kastin, 21, a waitress in Hollywood. She parked her green Volkswagen Beetle at the curb. Ken approached her while Angelo waited in the car. Like Judy, she was taken back to Angelo's. Angelo was disgusted, he could barely climax: Lissa went in for the "hippie" look and didn't shave her legs. Revolting. So he was especially rough on her, and tortured her after they were through with the sex. He would take the plastic bag off her head, giving her enough air to keep her alive a little longer, then tighten his hold until, after almost an hour, she finally died. Her body was found November 6, 1977.

Meanwhile, Ken had a girlfriend, Kelli Boyd, but he was losing interest in any sexual relationship with her. Just as in his Rochester days, he had found both good girls and bad girls. Kelli was "good," and so he lacked sexual desire for her. He was becoming less able to have sex with her. Seven months pregnant with his son, the young woman was having reservations of her own about the odd relationship. Ken had quit working, and told her and his most recent employer that he had cancer. He had been maintaining an office with a psychologist. He had purchased a fake certificate showing that he had a PhD, and he had actually talked his way into a shared office space and begun procuring clients. Now, with "cancer," Ken was free to spend more time with Angelo. Kelli was happy to have him out of the house, as he had become increasingly edgy.

On November 9, 1977, the killers cruised by a bus stop and noticed a lovely woman sitting on the bench, waiting for a ride. Ken told Angelo he wanted to handle this gal — no badges. He wanted to watch her put herself in the car.

Ken walked up, and began discussing Scientology and acting with her. She was interested in both subjects. Then Angelo pulled up and Ken ran to the car, feigning surprise. He went back to the woman, Jane King, and said that as luck would have it, his buddy "Tony" didn't mind offering them a ride. Jane happily agreed. They stopped at a convenience store and the men went inside, discussing their plan. They were giddy — she was gorgeous. The plan was going very much according to their pattern. Later, going through their usual procedures, they deviated from earlier patterns only in that they injected her with Windex and also took photos of themselves with her naked, half-dead body. And her shaved pubic region had spurred yet another bright idea with Angelo: he wanted the next victim to be young. A child.

At Eagle Rock Plaza, Ken approached Dolores Cepeda, 12, and Sonja Johnson, 14. Fatefully, they had just been shoplifting, so when Ken said he was "Security," they went with him without much surprise. They were sodomized, tortured and murdered. A 9-year-old boy found the Catholic students near Dodger's Stadium in mid-November.

The same day, the two found another victim — Ken's ex-neighbor, who had rejected his advances months before. Posing as a security guard, he knocked at her door and told her he'd ticketed her vehicle for parking illegally. She was brutalized with the vengeance born of Ken's sense of rejection. An honor student from the Pasadena Art Center of Design, her body was found near Ranon's Way and Wawona Hills (which separate Glendale from Eagle Rock). A worker clearing brush on the Los Felize Highway off-ramp near the Golden State Freeway found her body. Her distraught family is still trying to rebuild their lives in the wake of the horror and the publicity that followed.

Lauren Rae Wagner, 18, lived with her parents in the San Fernando Valley. She was simply crossing the street to get in her car when she had the misfortune of stumbling across the killing team. The media had, by now, dubbed the two "the Hillside Stranglers." Bodies kept being found, dumped on hillsides, and the police had figured out that more than one man was involved, since there were no signs of dragging the corpses, which a solo operator would have been forced to do.

Bianchi was relishing the publicity, but Angelo was getting nervous. He thought Ken was acting like an idiot. Why couldn't screwing and killing be enough? Why this need to see himself in the limelight? Ken tried to explain that every time he saw their names, he felt vindicated: the police had rejected his application to the LAPD, and he found a glory in outsmarting them now.

Kelli couldn't figure out what Ken was up to, but she had determined that he was not a fit father. She moved back to her hometown of Bellingham, Washington; Ken temporarily moved into a gay bathhouse. There, he bragged about the killers who were "smarter than the pigs." Ultimately, he was kicked out for using locally unacceptable profanity, such as "faggot"; but he accidentally left his everso-useful badge behind. It was handed over to the police. At first, there was fear that police officers might actually be involved in the murders; but the men living at the bathhouse mentioned their suspicions about Ken, reported where they thought he was living, and said that he'd been caught lying about being with the police department.

So the authorities went to interview him. They were moving in. Finally, they had a suspect. Angelo was furious. He warned Ken to get out of town. "Go to Kelli," he told him. Ken sullenly headed to Bellingham, and Kelli let him move in with her and their son, Sean. But it didn't last. She was getting ready to end their relationship for good when a knock came at her door. It was the police, and they wanted to search the house in relation to a double homicide that had occurred.

Ken had approached two girls he'd met at a supermarket, Fred Meyer's, where he'd had a temp job as a security watchman. He told the girls, Karen Mandic and Diane Wilder, that he'd gotten a side-job house-sitting for a family who lived in Bayside (an upper class area of the small, coastal town) and invited them over. The girls jumped at the chance and, arriving at the house, were met by Ken who offered to "show them around." Instead, he bludgeoned them to death. But this time, without Angelo, he couldn't get aroused.

Kenneth Bianchi stood over the battered bodies and tried to masturbate; finally he climaxed. He himself explains that he only was able to (achieve climax) *"by thinking of Angelo with him... it wasn't the same... it was so frustrating to have thought it would mean something but the whole thing meant nothing without him."* So that, in fact, Ken's excitement came less from the women and his participation in cutting short their lives and more from the sense of "accomplishment" and approval he derived from his cousin. His scheme to kill in Bellingham had been devised to prove to Angelo that he needed him back in Los Angeles, anyway. Bianchi was bored with small town life, and lonelier than he could imagine without Angelo.

In 48 hours, Bianchi was apprehended. By April of 1979 he was extradited back to Los Angeles to face charges as one of the Hillside

Stranglers. He incriminated his cousin in the crimes, but Angelo was calm, and never provided the police with any information. Angelo had married again and started a new life, and for a year had managed to keep a low profile. The trial was one of California's longest, and Bianchi received multiple murder counts while his cousin received only one. Bianchi was sent back to Washington State, to serve his sentence at Walla Walla, while Angelo Buono remains in California at San Quentin.

To add to the drama and tragedy, Bianchi took another victim during his stay at the men's county jail in Los Angeles. Veronica Compton, a budding actress and playwright, went to interview him. Using his latest scheme as a "victim of multiple personality," he blamed all his actions on Steve Walker, his alter-ego; and he was able to convince the 21-year-old writer that "Ken" was innocent. Veronica was suffering from a severe drug-induced psychosis at the time, and she did see Ken as a victim of his own mental disability. When Ken asked her to go and see his mother, to tell her that she had been with him on one of the alleged murder nights, Veronica obeyed. The next day, Ken's mother told officials of the conversation and forever after, the B-List talent was hailed as the killer's "girlfriend." Ken then told her (and only her) that he had lied about the multiple personality — he'd picked up the idea from a psychology book. But now, who would believe her? After all, she was "the Hillside Strangler's lover." Bianchi convinced her that he'd leave her alone — if she'd go to Bellingham and commit a "copycat killing" to get him off the hook. Veronica, under the influence of drugs, thought it was her last chance to free herself of this madman.

Disguised as a pregnant woman, she flew to Bellingham with a sample of Ken's semen, a rope tied like those he used at his crime scenes, and a tape with dialogue from an actor friend based on a "script" by Ken, saying that the police had the wrong man. Veronica found a victim, Kim Breed, in a cocktail bar. After chatting with the woman and giving her some drugs, Veronica took her back to her hotel room and proceeded to strangle her. Only — she couldn't. Falling to the floor, sobbing, she cried again and again, *"I can't, but Ken makes me do these things..."*

Still, the next morning before boarding a plane back to Los Angeles, Veronica gave a tape recording to the woman working at the ticket counter and asked her to pass it on to the police. The woman, thinking Veronica seemed odd, made sure the police got hold of the tape. The TV news that night asked the community of Bellingham if they'd dealt with any women or men who'd made mention of Kenneth Bianchi or the Hillside Stranglers. Kim called the police, and Veronica Compton found herself facing charges of attempted murder. Found guilty, her life has been spent at the Women's Correctional Center in Washington. She received the harshest prison sentence for attempted murder in the state's history. She is still dubbed the "Copycat Killer," although no one died as a result of her actions.

In one way or another, Ken Bianchi has continued to lure, manipulate and objectify women, whether he is behind bars or a free man. His ability to control women seems to transcend even cell walls. And yet, the only person he ever seemed to love or want to please was a man, his cousin Angelo Buono.

Officer Daniel Wright of the South San Francisco Police thought he was responding to a shoplifting call — nothing more, nothing less. But there, at South City lumberyard, he was the first authority present at the beginning of what turned into one of the most notorious, hideous investigations in United States history.

Officer Wright approached a 1980 Honda Prelude, where he met a large, bearded man and the store clerk (who had called after observing a man put a vise inside his jacket). The clerk explained that the man standing next to him had been accompanied by another man — a short, Asian fellow who'd run off. Officer Wright looked into the car and saw a bag containing what looked to be a handgun. He was right. There was a silencer, too. The large man tried to smooth things over, showing the officer a receipt and explaining that he'd paid for the vise his friend had taken and saying that the gun was registered to him.

"What about the car?" Officer Wright asked.

"It belongs to Lonnie Bond." The bearded man answered.

"Where is he?"

"Up north."

By now, the officer had run a check on the vehicle, only to find the Honda's registration number (838WFQ) belonged to a Buick. Swapping registrations was a crime. "I need to see some I.D.," the officer demanded. He asked if the man understood that silencers were also illegal.

"It's not mine. It belongs to Lonnie. I just use it to shoot beer cans," came the man's reply.

A check of the serial number, via radio, revealed that the weapon was registered to one Robin S. Stapley.

"You're under arrest."

"What for?"

"Owning an illegal weapon."

"I told you, it's not mine."

"You say your name is Stapley, right? The gun is registered in your name."

The officer handcuffed the man. The sales clerk was prudently standing some distance away. Wright put out a broadcast, based on the clerk's description of the Asian: male, slight of build, aged about 25, last seen wearing a parka. Wright locked "Stapley" into the backseat of his police car and drove his prisoner to South City police station, where he placed him in an interrogation room. The defendant was instructed to empty his pockets; among his possessions was a travel receipt in the name of Charles Gunnar. As one officer was asking "Who is Gunnar?," another officer was advising Wright that the vehicle identification number on the Honda revealed that it belonged to a man named Paul Cosner, who had been reported missing to the San Francisco Police nine months earlier. Officer Wright informed the bearded man that they had this information; the man turned ashen, and asked in a dull voice for a glass of water — and a pen and a pad.

While writing a "confession," the arrested man sipped the water. With it, he snuck down a small capsule. Good to have a little cyanide on hand for such an occasion. Leonard Lake was dead. So many questions, and no one alive — or, at least, on hand — to answer.

After fingerprints revealed Lake's true identity, officers were able to take a look at the mysterious man's past. It was ugly: a known criminal with a penchant for sex and paramilitary posturing. A review of his acquaintances proved that Lake's companion that day was Charles Ng (pronounced "ing"), who also had a long, sordid criminal history. Indeed, there had been a Robin Stapley; he had been reported missing several months earlier. As it turned out, several people who had touched one or the other man's life were now missing.

Inquiries led to Wilseyville, in Calaveras County outside the Sacramento Valley. Lake had maintained a ranch there. Investigators now set out to search the area for evidence; and evidence they found. Lake had dug a bunker into the hillside, and inside it he had constructed an elaborate torture chamber. Forensics experts found several pieces of evidence telling the terrible story of multiple rape, sexual assault and, apparently, murder. Pornographic books and photographs of nude women were strewn across the floor. The bunker area held the burnt remains of several human bodies, and a diary which would finally tell the story of Leonard Lake and Charles Ng, and this hideous house of horrors: "I want to control all women. I confess my desire to take women and own them. . . to make sex-slaves. . . kill women. . ."

Almost unbearable to watch, there were videotapes left as proof to back up Lake's words. The men had recorded themselves torturing women, raping them, forcing them to serve them. In some of the tapes, the men are laughing while the women, humiliated, stripped naked, are bringing things to them. One indescribable window into their cruelty shows us one woman being promised she'd have her baby boy back, as long as she "behaved." A boy, presumably hers, eighteen months old, was found burned and partially buried among many other victims in the bunker.

Immediately following the initial look-around, a warrant was issued for the still-missing Charles Ng, wanted on eleven counts of murder. No one knew that like Ng, like Lake, had his own plan. He was a "survivalist" (like Lake), and he was already in Canada. Ng seemed to have gotten away.

Incredibly, he began shoplifting again, in Calgary, and this time he did not manage to run. What is it in human psychology that would enable a person to commit the acts that Ng and Lake reveled in; and what leads a person with so much at stake to take further risks, knowing he cannot afford to be caught?

Charles Ng was faced with several dilemmas typical of a serial killer — he was filled with a sense of power, of being invincible; after all, he'd escaped California, and escaped going to prison despite the gruesome findings in Wilseyville. He figured he was smarter than everyone, and figured he therefore deserved anything he wanted: from a simple piece of hardware to a human life. It was all the same, to him. Charles Ng's behavior was learned, to some extent — including the instinct to survive, at all costs, that he picked up or fostered during military training. This, coupled with a history of childhood degeneracy, is the only explanation we have for his later lifestyle. He had an ability to take things and to capture women, and he validated his actions with the thought that he had a right to it all.

Ng and Lake force the reader down an uncomfortable path toward understanding the "why" behind crimes of murder. It is most unsettling that such crimes could be triggered by little more than a need to satiate a drive for power, a desire to "have." But that is just what is so horrific about these crimes, and the men and women who collectively commit them. As this book seeks to make plain, the dilemma then falls on society to learn what are the signs of a budding deviance, and to identify early on those people who are starting down questionable paths that may lead to lethal behaviors.

Unfortunately, society will not find the answers anytime soon; deviant behavior is here to stay. Furthermore, while some of the men and women who kill are intelligent, others are mentally less able, and most had dreadful childhoods. Difficult as it is to accept, they have a moral right to be affected by their pasts, just as society has a right (and an obligation) to intervene — to help children in trouble, as well as to curtail the activities of anyone who breaches the bounds of acceptable behavior. Is state-sponsored execution an answer? Actually, this most expedient way out is interpreted by killers and by society at large as a means of de-sensitizing us to murder in its many forms.

We are revolted by these unspeakable crimes, yet we must continue to look toward the profiles of the killer — all the things that, combined, created this inexplicable person. And we must take that profile, and move forward in our educational and judicial process, taking note always that these persons make up a subculture of their own. They live by different rules, and they have different mindsets, but they are penalized as if they were like "the rest of us." Here, we touch upon a crucial question: how are we to penalize such atrocity? How can we expect same-minded responses from the monsters of our culture when, in actuality, beyond any spiritual equation, they live in worlds so far from our own. These people do not look at legal sanctions in the same way that the rest of us might: murderers do not look at consequences. Certainly, they will try to evade capture (at any cost); but once caught, they will focus only on freedom (at any cost). The only time to really "catch" and "stop" these damaged souls is long before imprisonment is necessary.

By the time Charles Ng was found in Calgary, for example, he was very far beyond hope of rehabilitation. As Sgt. Neal of the Indiana Correctional Department said, at the time, "True rehabilitation begins at [age] three or four. The minute the signs of amoral behavior are demonstrated. Sadly, the behavior occurs behind closed doors, usually falling on either blind eyes or disinterested hearts."

In any case, Ng resisted capture and used his background in the military and training in the martial arts to fight back. He was overcome, eventually, and in due course was tried in Canada on charges of aggravated assault and robbery. He was convicted, and sentenced to four and a half years' imprisonment. Still, in his mind, he won: he had beat a system that could have taken his life. He would be able to own that sense of superiority for more than half a decade.

He resisted extradition to the U.S. for six years, until September, 1991, when he was finally flown back to California to face murder charges and the death penalty. Having shortened so many lives, Charles Ng now arrived at his own possible "termination" at the age of 30.

Ng had been born into a middle-class family in Hong Kong. At their wits' end after Charles had been expelled from several schools, his parents sent him to England to finish his education at Bentham boarding school. At 18, he traveled to the U.S. and floated around sunny California before enlisting in the Marines in 1979. His rebellious nature was still ruling his life; he was arrested in 1981 for stealing weapons and explosives from the Corps armory. He managed to elude prison, and it was while on the lam that he met up with a kindred soul, Leonard Lake.

As has been noted, murder teams usually comprise one dominating personality and at least one weaker personality. In this case, experts assess that Charles Ng was more than ripe for the life of torture, rape, and murder that he and Leonard Lake engaged in, but it was Lake who chose a specific path of sexual deviance. Combining details of his history with psychological profiling, Ng's schoolmates and public officials reckon that although Ng was obsessed with martial arts, he exhibited no signs of sexual pathology. On the other hand, Lake used his militant philosophies to back up a sado-sexual perversion. Charles had no scruples about lending Leonard a hand, and inflicting pain was all in keeping with his training. If Leonard wanted to satiate a sexual need, this did not conflict with his companion's ideology — which simply placed loyalty above all else.

It has been speculated that, similar to other killer teams, Lake and Ng on their own were degenerate, but it was only their combined personality that added up to a brutal killer: a disastrous example of what psychologists label Gestalt — when the organized whole is greater than the sum of its parts. Whatever the psychological facts may be, Ng's April 1992 trial ended with conviction and a death sentence. He sits at San Quentin, ten years later, still waiting.

Jenny,

Toward the end of my killing spree, I became very bold and aggressive in my abductions. Why, I'm not sure. But it was like the more I did it, the more I thirsted for it.

People have asked me how could I do such horrible things to someone... what they didn't understand was I had shut off all my feelings and emotions. A woman to me became simply an object. And I suppose that to say I literally hunted women would be accurate.

You know, Jenny, I had absolutely no desire of any kind to hurt a young child, boy or man. In fact, I went out of my way to abduct women who didn't have a child. That's why I was affected by the little baby. Although I abducted housewives with husbands, I didn't have any feelings toward the husband. I hunted hitchhikers a lot... If I liked a woman on a personal level, and I considered her a friend, she was off limits and I would even be protective of her. That's why people have told me none of this made sense... I wasn't what people think of when they think "serial killer."

David Gore

As hard as it is to fathom, he's right. He is not at all the sort of man that comes to mind when we try to imagine what a serial killer might be like. David Gore, unlike his cousin and killing partner, Fred, considered me a woman he "liked," and as he says in the letter above, I was therefore off-limits. We talked about his crimes, and much more. At times, I would have to take the phone from my ear, or put down his letter, and remind myself that this man had skinned women alive. Thrown women to alligators — alive. He had dismembered, sodomized, beaten, buried, kidnapped and murdered women, again and again, and he would have continued, if not for one single mistake. At least, that was the final analysis. And that is the pattern of a serial killer — like an alcoholic with a bottle at hand, the next "shot," the relapse, is inevitable. Take the shot, inhale the scent and repeat the ritual. . . the slow, welcome burn down the throat and smooth sense of intoxication and pleasure, and once again, the alcoholic is dry. He looks in the mirror and shakes his head, as confused by his addiction as anyone.

Gore reminds me of the alcoholic. He speaks like someone who has taken responsibility for his inexplicable past, one filled with brutality and murder. He never makes threats or suffers from inconsistencies in mood. . . but give him his freedom, and he would become, again, very much a serial killer-a-hol-ic. Like most serial killers, take away the temptation and the perpetrator becomes quite a functional part of a prison community. Put him back into society, and the killing cycle begins again; and he may be as confused as anyone about why he *had* to do it.

David Gore grew up in a rural area of Florida, not far from Vero Beach, and he was still there as an adult living a normal, family life. It was there that he'd become a valued member of the business community. And there that he would commit a series of killings with his cousin, Fred Waterfield, his only friend while growing up in the middle of nowhere.

Many question which came first. Was David a bad seed, destined to become a murderer, or was it only because he had spent so many years alone with a deviant influence that allowed him to entertain dark thoughts, becoming less sensitized to the value of a woman's life? Having researched their lives and corresponded with both members of this team, I would guess that, without the dominant characteristics and the power of persuasion that Fred Waterfield possessed, David Gore is not likely to have landed himself on death row in a Florida penitentiary. As statistics prove, many passive team members have no criminal history before their partnering with the "leader." Gore reinforces that theory with his own "clean" past; without Fred's infiltrating his thoughts and ultimately his actions, he might never have resorted to violence as a way to deal with women, whom he held responsible for damaging — even destroying — his life.

When David and Fred were both about 13 years old, Fred suggested that they rape their mothers. There weren't many girls out in the countryside, and according to Fred, a mother was still a woman. David was shocked, but his shy nature disallowed him to say no; rather, he silently prayed Fred had only been kidding. One never knew with Fred. David had already stood witness to his cousin's rape of a young girl who rode their same school bus. Anything was possible.

Fred Waterfield was popular, something that was missing from his cousin's life. At school, Fred wasn't known to be deviant. He was well-liked, charismatic and fairly good-looking. He never had a problem getting a date, but often told David that women were scum, and "only good for getting fucked," David explained to me in a letter, describing his cousin

By contrast, David was on the hunt for a relationship. He shared none of his cousin's confidence in a group, yet he didn't like being alone. He longed for someone to care about him. Of course, with no one but Fred as a friend, he kept his less macho thoughts to himself — it was that, or be rejected.

Graduation came and went, and while Fred skipped from one girl and one prom to the next, his cousin left high school empty-handed. Moving to Vero Beach, he found that finally there were women out there who found him interesting. All the popularity games from rural no-man's-land meant nothing. And David finally met a woman. Like a fairytale, David married and had two sons.

Still, Fred came around with his relentless, negative attitude toward women. Now, it wasn't simply awkward for David, it was a point of contention between him and his wife. But how could David turn his back on a lifelong family relation? It seemed that with each passing day, the pressure increased, with Mrs. Gore insisting that David make Fred Waterfield go away. One day, the turning point came: Fred or me. Something inside of David boiled. Had Fred been right about women? How could his own wife make such a demand on him? And what right did any woman have to call the shots, anyhow? His mind whirled. His back against a wall, he became defiant, and challenged her in return. The result was a divorce.

David's rage escalated. He became physically and mentally abusive. In court, his wife was able to prove that David was at least temporarily out of control. The judge awarded his now ex-wife full custody of their two sons. The boys were the only two beings David had ever loved unconditionally — from fishing trips to homework, David had been a wonderful father. Even his ex-wife won't dispute that, today. In fact, she'll add that he also provided a solid income for the family. But what Donna Gore had hoped would serve as a temporary "time-out," enforced by the courts, was construed by her husband as an absolute abandonment. If any seeds had been planted early on, they were in gestation now. . . David was ready to join the anti-female campaign, aka the Fred Waterfield club.

Together, and sometimes alone, they began to lure women.

David volunteered as a reserve deputy with the Vero Beach Sheriff's Department; the I.D. card and badge came in handy. Sometimes, the men raped, then let their victims go, alive. Other women weren't so lucky. More of a "maintenance drinker" than an "alcoholic," somehow Fred managed to keep things under wraps. He worked, he raped, sometimes he killed; but he was never out of control. David, on the other hand, became more and more vengeful. His resentment toward his wife was not only displaced on all women, but each victim got a more plentiful dose of hate during the rape and/or murder. He found that with his killings, he somehow had a sense of momentary "relief," as he describes. He explained (in a letter to me, in 1997) that he felt like a man suffocating under the laws, the restrictions, the hate toward his wife, Donna. "And that when (he) killed, those horrible senses would dissipate — at least, temporarily."

David even killed his own sister-in-law. Under the guise of getting together for a cup of coffee, he went to visit her. Somewhat reluctantly, she allowed him into her home. He bludgeoned her, raped her while she was semi-conscious, and then put her in the back of his camper truck. He drove her to some acreage he owned, with a small barn-like structure; and inside, he suspended her by her ankles where a deer was meant to hang, to be skinned. Incredibly, on this day, a human being would hang, and one who had shared many moments in his life.). In spite of her pleas and tears, skin her he did. She eventually collapsed into unconsciousness, in shock and pain, and finally died. According to court transcripts, autopsy reports completed in Vero Beach determine that she bled to death. In front of her body, still hanging head down, Gore masturbated. He felt control, he explained to me years later. Never again would a woman control his destiny. Gore was plagued by what he deemed to have been his own stupidity. How could he have been so naïve about these conniving women? Fred had been right all along.

After approximately twelve (documented) murders came a

time when Gore and Waterfield were holding two girls, Lynne Elliott and Regan Martin, captive at Gore's home. They raped both of them. Lynne took her chances and seized a moment to run out the front door, still naked. Gore chased her down and shot her in the head, killing her. A neighbor witnessed the event and Gore and Waterfield were apprehended. Little Regan Martin was found huddled, nude, in a corner near the kitchen.

Ironically, while the witness was calling 911, so was David Gore. In 1983, after years of murder and hatred, David was "too tired to carry on." The court took little pity on a man whose "fatigue" materialized so late in the game and on March 10, 1984, David Gore was sentenced to die. He waits for execution at the Union Correctional Institution in Raiford, Florida. Waterfield, turning evidence on his cousin, was sentenced to life in prison.

It was only luck, and Ms. Elliott's courage despite sheer terror, that finally caused someone to see Gore in mid-attack. No one will ever know if his story is true: that he was too tired to kill anymore, anyway. Perhaps the media slant is more accurate: a smart man, he knew when he was caught. Better to turn himself in, since a man full of remorse has a better chance of escaping the death penalty than one who is unrepentant. The courts obviously agreed that this was a canny, not candid, position for Gore, and he did not escape the death penalty.

Whatever reason he had for aiding in his own apprehension, calculated or not, today Gore provides us something few serial killers ever do: facts and details and honest accounts. They are too much to bear. But Gore has a lot to get off his chest. He recognizes that he "will meet his Maker," he explains. He wonders if even Christ can find it in his angelic heart to forgive a man who committed such unspeakable acts, over and over and over. Alone in a cramped cell, having visited ruthless terror upon so many individuals, Gore ponders his mortality with fear, everyday. And while much of what Gore says is only grounds for speculation, this I know to be true.

# PART IV
## FAMILY AND GROUP KILLERS

Team killers often have unexciting reasons for committing their crimes. Waltraud Wagner was clearing her ward of patients who disrupted her sense of control; Charles Manson wanted to get back at the police, and rock musicians, and to become "a name." Other groups may act out of ethnic hatred, or out of extreme political beliefs. A case in point is the Zebras, who — taking to its extreme the belief system expounded by the Black Panthers in the 1970s — decided that any white person: man, woman or child — deserved to be dead.

Oftentimes, what begins as an earnest political statement is taken to extremes, and taken out of context, by people who join a group with different motives in mind — deviant fantasies, illusions of grandeur and power, or even a desire to discredit and bring down the group in question. Anti-establishment actions that may once have had a purpose, however laudable or debatable, can run amok and devolve (or be led) into thrill killing.

The Zebra killings were, at least at first, motivated by racist hatred. This is a ghastly example of prejudice gone haywire. The perpetrators were all Black. The collective crime spree took place over 179 days.

At the core of the Zebra "family" were five men who considered themselves elite assassins and took the name, "Death Angels." More prosaically, they were ex-convicts: Jesse Cooke, Larry Greene, Anthony Harris, JC Simon and Manuel Moore. They'd already committed crimes in the name of Black supremacy, proclaiming a desire to annihilate White "devils." And even in their worst crimes, the Black Muslims (a political and controversial group at best) supported the Zebras. The Zebras were highly organized: California authorities were investigating the murders of 135 white men, 75 white women and 60 white children. It was the randomness of the crimes (the only link being skin color) that led police to believe the assassinations had been committed by the Zebras.

Membership in the group required killing at least 9 white men, 5 white women or 4 white children. That was the only requirement;

racial hatred was enough. Aspiring Zebra wannabe's were indoctrinated at special meetings and went to work throughout certain
parts of California, especially San Francisco. They patrolled in two's
and three's, randomly "hitting" White people at bus stops, laundro-
mats, parking lots and telephone booths. In addition, going beyond
the prescribed model, they raped one white woman and abducted a
man whom they then tortured and butchered, alive.

The killings soon escalated beyond the realm of "political
statement" into the realm of thrill killings. The public was in a
panic; this massive underground operation seemed to have a grip on
most of the urban districts of San Francisco, creating even more friction between minorities and the Law.

In early 1974, investigators blanketed the Black communities;
literally thousands of blacks were taken off the streets and questioned at police headquarters. Finally, Anthony Harris, one Zebra
member, chronicled some of the more grisly events in his own de-
tailed confession, which implicated four of his collaborators. May 1,
1974 was marked by 100 police officers storming through apartment
blocks throughout the city. Seven arrests were made. A small number but, as it happens, enough for starters.

While the Black Muslims could not be held accountable for
inspiring the Zebra murders, these arrests laid the groundwork for a
trial of those directly involved the assassination of fifteen men,
women and children in late 1973 and the beginning of 1974 (eight
more victims, also all White, were seriously wounded — three of
them paralyzed for life). This would become one of California's
longest and most historical legal battles, lasting a year and six days.
The trial began before Supreme Court Judge Joseph Koresh on
March 3, 1975. Anthony Harris was not tried, as he'd turned state's
evidence. One hundred eighty one witnesses were called, and Anthony Harris spent twelve days on the stand, testifying.

A unanimous verdict of guilty was ultimately achieved, resulting in life sentences for all four defendants. Two served out their sentences at Folsom Prison, two at San Quentin. Twenty years after the sentencing, one of them wrote to me about his life in prison. His letter offers a glimpse into the minds of those who got caught up in the action. He wishes to remain anonymous.

*When we struck out against the whites, you would have to know the times. I mean, Angela Davis was a Black Panther, and today she's probably one of your friends. How would you have felt, knowing she used to toss Molotov Cocktails? We were in a frenzy, and it wasn't right — it was me taking out my anger, with this perfect cult-like group supporting me. . . all of us, you know? I hated whites, whites hated blacks. Most of us weren't buying into this free-love thing, because the truth was always the same, we occupied the ghettos, there were no ways to get our asses up the ladder. There was anger everywhere. And you can think what you want, but radical actions was part of those times. The movies and the organizations. . . it was like an invitation to be crazy with being pissed off. When I arrived here, to start my time, I was really pissed. I been in and out of these places, and I thought a lot of me killing was like getting rid of the reason why I ever had to end up in here in the first place. I was angry a long time. I still won't talk about some of that, because maybe I'll always be angry, knowing that people get away with racism everyday, and then. . . well, you know. I'm here. But the biggest truth is, I deserved it. I ain't going nowhere. So I'm not feedin you this. I know this is it, and I'll die. But it doesn't have to be as bad, now, because the beating stop, the prejudice don't exist, now, really. There are groups of different people, who hang together, protect each other from other gangs and even guards. That was really hard at first. Guards. 'Cause they were so scared of me, so ready to pounce like I was an animal. But hey — I was an animal. I had to be stopped. You know, just cause a kid was white, could be doing nothing wrong, just feeding ducks for all I cared, but the membership meant so much, so I would just walk up and fire. Kill, baby! and think nothing. 'Cause I'd go back to a meeting and people would clap. It makes you feel part of something, and all that praise makes you feel like you did something very good. Everything gets way messed up. So I have to live with some of that, and I go to sleep and that part, the assassinations feel like I just done one, but I know it's been a long time. Shit, I could have been something else. Too bad, but I make all I can out of this. I try never to let myself be around the people who go 'oh, that guys a spic so let's knife him or something.' No more. And I don't let myself get drawn into a group 'cause they accept me 'cause I'm black and that's all. That's where I got into trouble. Like being in some club where no one is invited but you and a few other special people. Really it ain't nothing except the skin. That's making me shake my head, just watching myself writing down. It's good to say this, sorry about my name. But I could get in trouble, on both sides, you know. So remember, tell those folks out there that if you got to hate, find something to hate for real. When you think of that, [there's] not too much worth hating and it always ends up you being the one in trouble. Being with the wrong people or whatever. It took years to recover my reputation. I was every-thing from a fuck to the nigger boy that got the beatings. Now I'm just me, and that's the past. Sometimes I think on that, too. That could maybe make me hate, but I could hate me for taking out a kid, or some mom. So I just try and make my life worth living, even if it's behind walls. It's possible. And then letters still come, like yours, and make me think: I owe the world something, some explanations. So if that's all I got, then I'll give it. So thanks. Bye.*

*Respectfully,*

*X.*

Journal Entry, January 8, 1997

*I took Eddie Spreitzer's call outside, on the portable. I had a feeling that I didn't even want his dreadful energy in my home — and then I talked to him. I had read his C sheet (prison report), which listed an IQ of 71. I realized this put him far beneath standards of normalcy, but I never would have thought that he would be unable to grasp the magnitude of his crimes. He had blood work done today (performed on death-row inmates, on a regular basis) and he fainted. His counselor said he always faints when he sees blood.*

*I asked Eddie about this, how it related to being able to sever a breast? "Sever? What's that mean?" I thought he was toying with me. Then he started to cry. He said he thinks he knows that the women are dead. He asks me if I know for certain. ["His mental incapacity prohibits Edward Spreitzer's truly understanding mortality," says Dr. Ian Moran, the professional profiler from Riverside, California, who has worked with Spreitzer]. "Do those girls get to come back? I mean, they wasn't all buried so did maybe some live?"*

*He's barely able to articulate his words, and he's crying. He goes on to tell me about the time he was showering, after first brought to Pontiac (the men's prison) and "some 30 guys rape me. I had about 300 stitches in my butt but even though I fainted, then I woke up." So he thinks maybe if he survived something that ripped him apart, made him bleed and faint, then maybe the women he hurt would recover, too. "No, Eddie. You helped kill them. They don't get to come back." He can't do anything but sob. So I'm sitting there, my hands freezing and I'm wishing I had my mittens on. Mostly I'm shaking from fear, not the cold, because here I am empathizing with a man who killed so many women, and how would that make my friends feel. . . like I was a nut case. But you had to hear this to know it was genuine. I know the other gang members, too. I know which ones are conning me, and this one isn't.*

*"They'll kill me, and I'm really afraid. I don't want to die. I'm very scared to die, Miss Jenny."*

*I am talking to a mentally-retarded man who was sucked into the Ripper gang and can't even dissect what he's done, or the consequences. I felt like I might cry, myself. Maybe I was just cold, or short of sleep — no, the truth is, I felt horrible. Spreitzer is not in the right place. He doesn't belong with hardened criminals. His actions were born of dangerous leadership and his inclination to follow. If they had said he could fly, he would have said, "Great,'" and jumped off a cliff. At least, for the time being, Illinois has put a stay on executions.*

*I called Spreitzer's mother today, explaining that the Governor just released Kruz on a wrongful conviction, and with television appearances coming, perhaps with her help we could bring him some attention, hopefully have him transferred to a more appropriate institution. Imagine, a dozen people were wrongfully killed last year, in one state alone. Illinois has put in place a stay on any further executions after DNA tests proved that misuse of forensic evidence had led to 13 wrongful deaths/executions. I'm glad for this attention to the issue of capital punishment, but what about this man who should be a mental patient, but is locked up in a prison for the sane? He's clearly not capable of grasping anything much beyond a sixth grade level. His mother says she realizes these things are true, that Eddie went through eighth grade three times, and then his stepfather kicked him out of their mobile home, in the snow, with no shoes; and after a couple of years on the streets, he ended up with the Ripper gang.*

*What a perfect guy for a bunch of sadists — until he goes in and confesses. He says, "I think we done something really wrong." And they're on him like he's the ringleader, evil. Without him, they'd still be searching for bodies. He does deserve to be put away, but differently — he is so suggestible; he should have been put away long ago, as a danger to himself and to others. Drinking problems, can't read... no one notices a 17-year-old who can't read, so here we are. I'm having a conversation with a man who wonders what death is.*

*And his mother can only say, "Yes, I know, I know... we didn't do right by him. But the marriage, I don't want to do anything to upset the marriage. Eddie used to upset it — make my husband so angry. I feel bad Eddie ran, and I know my husband was partly responsible, he was so "corporal." But our lives have settled. I don't want to cause any disruption." I tell her that a "stay" can be dismissed, and Eddie's up for death, here. Just a few words about his disability and his childhood hardships to ensure that he isn't killed? "No, no... I just can't do that." So she'd let him die — that's the kind of "nurturing" that helped send him to the Rippers in the first place. What can possibly go so wrong, that a mother could be so detached from her own child? I'm at an emotional loss.*

Never had the Windy City been struck by such violence as it was in 1981 and 1982. Chicago police could only compare the nightmarish murders that occurred in that time frame with those committed by Jack the Ripper in turn-of-the-century London.

Women were being discovered dead throughout the city: prostitutes, but also "career" girls. People were terrified to leave their homes; the killings were unspeakably gruesome. Later, connections to gang killings of men were also linked to the perpetrators, but the case formally opened with the murder of Linda Sutton. A black prostitute, she was attacked in May 1981. Forced into a van, she was told to drink from a Coke bottle, which was filled with mashed-up pills — tranquilizers. Once incapacitated, her abusers raped her, then performed an "operation" of sorts on the woman: they severed her left breast. Her body was further mutilated, then she was gang-raped and stabbed to death.

One year later, two other women would die in separate incidents. Lorraine Borowski, a young and ambitious assistant at a real estate company was abducted while letting herself into her offices early one morning in 1982. Shui Mak disappeared while walking home after working at her family's Chinese restaurant. She'd told her brother that she was in love with a white man (a show against tradition in this old-fashioned Chinese family), and they had a fight, in their car. The parents were in another car, ahead of them on the road. Shui became distraught and got out of the car at a stoplight. A van pulled up next to her, and she was never seen again. Eddie Spreitzer knows best what happened to her:

"We took her to the forest. And then we tied her to a tree. We cut off her breast and all that. I got back in the van and thrown up. Then I drunk some and past out. I know she was made to have sex with."

In August, the body of Sandra Delaware was found, strangled, with the "signature" severed left breast. Her body lay in the north tributary of the Chicago River. The attacks, though all linked by similarities, were escalating in savagery.

Rose Beck was a young sales representative, out for dinner at a Chicago hotel. As she walked to her car in the covered parking lot, she was approached by four men in a van. She put up a fight, which seemed to amuse her killers. Her attack was particularly brutal. She was raped, bludgeoned, axed through the torso, stabbed several times, and strangled; both breasts were mangled with a knife.

Finally, in September of 1982, another victim was abducted, forced to take tranquilizers, raped, and had her breast severed. She was tossed from the van after the attack; she lay in a pool of her own blood, but somehow, she lived. Taken to a local hospital, the 18-year-old prostitute recuperated and was able to provide a description of her assailants, the van and its interior.

Three nights later, a patrol car pulled up next to a red van fitting the description given by the survivor. Its occupants, Eddie Spreitzer, 20, and his 19-year-old "buddy" Andrew Kokoraleis, were questioned. Eddie told the officers that the vehicle belonged to Robin Gecht, his employer. He explained the tools in the back of the van as belonging to the construction company his employer owned. The contents included an axe, rope and several knives. The police weren't buying.

The young men were taken into custody for further questioning. Within the hour, Edward Spreitzer was confessing to his part in a vicious crime spree. Robin Gecht was picked up next, but denied any involvement, claiming Spreitzer was "retarded" and "didn't know what he was talking about." The police were able to detain Gecht, in spite of his professed innocence, on a previous count of sexual assault and several charges of abusive behavior. He was a suspect, whether he liked it or not. Police noted how cool and calm Robin Gecht seemed. He was relaxed, his legs crossed and his demeanor casual. He joked about the irony of his previous employment for John Wayne Gacy. It was true: Robin Gecht had worked for the serial killer, but John had taken a "special interest" in Robin — deciding to spare his life.

Andrew and Eddie were less calm. Between November 5 and 8, the pair disclosed information about victims, sites and circumstances. They also confessed to Andrew's brother's involvement, and Thomas Kokoraleis was brought down to the precinct. One year younger than his brother, he was more calculating than Andrew — he adamantly denied the stories of murder and mayhem. But Andrew continued to provide information. He admitted that an unsolved slaying of a man the year before had been "one of (ours)." He described their rituals, which included cannibalism. Eddie broke down, admitting that he had been told by Robin "that to be part of the group, he had to take a bite out of one of the breasts."

Gecht was defiant. He still is: "This is a barbaric attempt on the part of the worst legal system in the US — Illinois — to once again kill an innocent person. They'd love to kill me. But I'm innocent." His daughters agree. They stand by him, and bring his grandchildren to see him at Menard Penitentiary, where he serves 120 years for attempted murder and rape. This has become his weapon, that he couldn't be pinned to murder: "Even in their finest hour, they couldn't prove it was me. They tried to beat it and rape it out of me, but it wasn't me. Still, I may not have gotten the death sentence, but they know they're killing me in here." Robin has undergone bypass surgery since his incarceration and suffers hypertension. Few outsiders feel empathetic.

Meanwhile, the three other conspirators were sentenced to die; Andrew has already faced his execution. Thomas's sentence was reversed on a technicality, and plea-bargaining before his second trial got him a lesser sentence of seventy years' imprisonment.

Eddie still faces death. While the crimes are atrocious, Eddie's mental incapacity poses the question of inappropriate placement. Experts agree that Edward has no real sense of his participation in the crimes. In his mind, explains Dr. Crintz, psychologist, "He had been welcomed into a family. He still thinks these rituals were about bonding — not about killing. When you ask him if he killed, he doesn't know how to define the permanency of that."

I talked with Eddie, and it is true: he asked me himself, "Are they really dead?" Eddie did not face the challenge of the McNaughton standard of insanity*. That would have placed him in a mental institution. But clearly it was not an issue of insanity, but of disability. There is no "standard" for disability. And so he serves his sentence at Pontiac with people who do realize what they've done. His circumstance is pathetic. And if the stay of execution is overturned again, Eddie will surely face his Maker in the very near future.

---

*The McNaughton standard was established in the 1800's and is still the only criterion available to establish a legal defense on the grounds of insanity. The standard holds that it must be clearly proved that, at the time the act in question was being committed, the party was laboring under such a defect of reason, from disease of the mind, as to not know the nature and quality of his actions, or, if he did know it, that he did not know that what he was doing was wrong. (From *Murder Most Rare*, Michael Kelleher, p. 161. Praeger Publishers, 1998.)

## THE LAINZ HOSPITAL MURDERS

Forty-eight-year-old Stephania Mayer was a recently divorced grandmother in need of a job, after emigrating from her husband's homeland, Yugoslavia, back to Austria, where she was born in 1939. The marriage and divorce had both been sour; she could not rely on her husband for support. Immediately upon her arrival in Vienna, she began searching for work.

Luckily, in a matter of days, the Lainz Hospital responded to her application and offered her a nurse's aide position on the night shift. The hospital had an excellent reputation and a staff of 2,000. Built in 1839, the institution held a proud reputation as one of the most masterful medical institutions in the world. Mayer was over-joyed — not only to be employed, but to have received a position at this prestigious hospital. She was determined to make a good impression on her employers and her co-workers.

Waltraud Wagner was the chief nurse's aide for the ward to which Mayer was assigned. She was a 28-year-old Austrian. Pavilion Five was hectic, but Wagner had worked the unit almost five years and had warranted commendation for her calm under stress. One supervisor, during a subsequent interview, said she was "not only reliable, and efficient, but her authoritative skills were monumental. Her staff seemed to have a balanced respect and liking for her."*

Her peers saw Wagner slightly differently. Some agree that she was indeed experienced, but considered that her mostly aggressive, domineering behavior was a shortcoming — for both her staff and her patients.

Wagner introduced her newest employee to two young nurse's aides, Maria Gruber and Irene Leadoff, and they looked up to Stephania as a motherly figure; to them, 20 years younger, she embodied competence (although she had little experience as a nurse's aide). After a self-defeating marriage and a long struggle with self-esteem, Stephania enjoyed the respect of her co-workers. She was creating a niche for herself. And that became even easier when she was suddenly indoctrinated into the other workings of the Lainz Hospital's night shift staff.

Her damaged ego and her submissive behavior, born from years of difficult relationships, left her easily manipulated. It turned out that the night staff had tacitly evolved into a killing team. Waltraud Wagner had committed her first murder at barely 24 years of age, in 1983. She had been caring for a 77-year-old woman who was admitted to Pavilion Five on her last breath. As is common with terminal patients, she begged her nurse to end her torment. Eventually, the aide agreed to help her die. Wagner injected the elderly woman with an overdose of morphine.

Wagner couldn't believe how simple the murder was. No one suspected a thing — the body was quickly removed to the morgue,

---

*From *Murder Most Rare*, Michael Kelleher, *op. cit.*

and the ward was too busy to take special notice of what appeared to be a routine death. There was no suspicion whatsoever. A feeling of intense power surged through Wagner; she felt a supreme sense of self, founded in her ability to determine when (and when not) to take life — and it was so easy. Thus began her career in serial murder, which would continue for six years and would involve three accomplices, often operating by "remote control."

Maria Gruber was five years her junior, and Irene Leidolf three. Both were vulnerable to their dominant supervisor; Stephania Mayer was older and considerably more seasoned, but the calculating eye of a killer saw her as a highly suggestible person. And that is why she was approached immediately after being hired, and asked to become part of this subculture of killers.

A major footnote is the unique methodology employed here: a serial killer team leader executed plans, but didn't always murder, forcing the other members to commit the acts for the dominant figure. In serial killing families or groups, this is not unique. This was not difficult to achieve for Waltraud; the women were both frightened of her, and in awe of her power.

Waltraud was methodical in creating the operative dichotomy, whereby her subordinates feared and needed her at the same time. She kept an "umbrella" over her team, always knowing their movements, their daily activities. When Stephania Mayer came to Lainz, Waltraud had gone far beyond her initial morphine kill. She was now carrying out far more gruesome murders. One tactic was the "water cure." Similar to a torture originating during the Spanish Inquisition, the nurses would force water into the throats and lungs of their victims, forcibly drowning the helpless patients. Mostly, she stuck to lethal injections (which were safest from detection), but her own deviancy forced her to "experiment."

The nurses were controlled by her strict demand to know their whereabouts. They often discussed the crimes with one another, and mostly with an air of bragging, because they desperately wanted to please their leader. Each of the nurses acting for Waltraud was also in fear for her own life; after all, the patients were picked for murder because, in some way, they had crossed her — either by lodging a complaint or because they had demanded too much attention. Complaining to her or about her would incur a death sentence. Sometimes, in cases that had really annoyed her, she enjoyed terminating the "irritant" herself.

By 1988, one year after Stephania had joined the team, the deaths had become so commonplace that Pavilion Five was becoming suspect. Unfortunately for the four murderess-caretakers, coworkers had overheard their "discussions." They had begun to feel a sense of accomplishment in their deeds, since their leader praised them; and a sense of catharsis was provided when the three came together to talk about their crimes.

On February 11, 1989, the four women took their ramblings to the next level, drinking a little too much and spilling stories of murder a little too loudly. It happened that a team of Lainz hospital physicians was at a table nearby. One doctor, pondering the rumors about the ward that had circulated during the past year, excused himself from his table and immediately contacted the police. Officials confronted the physician in charge of Pavilion Five, Xavier Pesendorfer. He was dismissed as a suspect, but when he refused to help with the investigation, it only served to fuel the investigator's curiosity about the well-shielded unit.

The police realized they were going to receive no inside support, but they were determined to look into the odd, and a little too frequent, deaths that occurred. On April 9, 1989, just two months into the inquiry, evidence was established leading to the four women involved. Senior Investigator Franz Pressnitz held a press conference that shocked the media and the public, terrifying both with an unbelievable story of murder uncovered at this highly regarded institution. For his passive participation, Pesendorfer was removed from his position — a direct response to pressures put on the hospital by the public at large.

On the day that the doctor was suspended, an incredible confession came from Waltraud Wagner. She confessed to almost 40 murders, which she claimed to have committed alone. Taking her lead, the three others confessed to an additional ten killings, each. The detectives ordered that bodies of the patients listed in these confessions be exhumed to provide prosecutors with forensic evidence to build a stronger case.

That was an intelligent choice, considering that Wagner recanted her confession a couple of weeks later. It was too late: all the forensics evidence was in place, and Wagner's fate lay in the hands of the lifeless patients who had been placed in her trust. There was no question of guilt, only, guilty how many times over?

An exhaustive and exhausting investigation left prosecutors frustrated; their hands were tied for the next year while the body count was under way. The Lainz Hospital finally provided its own investigative research, allowing that as many as 200 deaths may have been related to the killers; but over seven years had passed, and the stories from each member of the team, which had been vague enough to begin with, had changed many times over. The investigation was becoming a dizzying maze of loosely constructed theories and dead ends. Prosecution wanted a conviction, and suggested that although additional cases could be uncovered, the deaths confirmed so far were horrific enough to warrant putting the public and the families at peace with a trial and sentencing.

On February 28, 1991 the four women finally went to trial, facing 42 counts of murders and multiple counts of attempted murder. Waltraud Wagner was first to take the stand, confessing both to lethal injections and the "water cure." As predicted, her followers took her lead, confessing to their murders. Prosecutors were looking at the most infamous case in Vienna's history, with recorded confessions and forensics to ensure harsh penalties.

On March 29, 1991, the perpetrators were each found guilty on all counts. Wagner and Leidolf were both sentenced to life in prison without parole. In Austria, this is the maximum penalty. Gruber and Mayer received a minimum of fifteen years in prison for attempted murder.

Later reports would show that the foursome perpetrated as many as 300 murders at Lainz Hospital. Austria had seen its most notorious trial in peace time, and the magically lovely, eminently civilized city of Vienna, famed for its opera balls and ballet-dancing horses, was revealed to have served as the stage for quite a different kind of performance: by the most prolific female serial-killing team in history.

## THE MANSON FAMILY

In the United States, the Manson trial may not make it onto the list of the most costly — or even most infamous — when compared to those of serial killer Ted Bundy, or Richard Ramirez, or perhaps John Wayne Gacy. However, within the realm of cult killers, the Manson family murders rank among the most well-known (universally) and the most shocking. The crimes committed by this "family" were unparalleled by other serial killers, acting alone or in teams.

Ironically their leader, Charles Manson (currently serving a life sentence and suspected in at least a dozen murders still categorized as "unsolved") has eluded the ultimate convictions and punishments his admirers and followers have faced. His puppets did his dirty work, proudly and with purpose, and they paid the price.

I exchanged letters with, and had access to, this man who persuaded others to torture and kill, creating a horror that burdened our society with a new and profound fear. But I felt that there was no revelation to be gained by sharing the contents of that corre-spondence — until I began writing this work. This maniacal man appeared to enjoy my attentions almost as much as his own ram-blings, and at least until the topic of team killers became an issue, it seemed worse than useless to provide Charles Manson with more of what he's always been obsessed with — notoriety.

My goal in presenting these cases to the reader is to provide an element of education, some window through which we can look to gain at least some degree of understanding of the causes of violence. By contrast, to allow Manson a voice on paper would only have meant promoting his discombobulated and self-indulgent narcis-sism, denial and, most important, his blatant contempt for his vic-tims, including both the persons who died at his own hand (pre-Manson Family, Charles is strongly implicated in additional mur-ders) and those who died at his commandment (during the Manson Family era, all he admits to even now is the "power of suggestion").

Who was Charles Manson, that he could become so infamous a killer, and why? His life history certainly meets the criteria that sometimes lead one to a life of crime: documented circumstances of the sort that are considered mitigating — a prostitute mother who abandoned him before his sixth year, long stints in a reformatory, then a brief period of freedom which led him to his place in history as one of the most mesmerizing "leaders" of all time. Manson's only "gift" became everyone else's nightmare: his innate ability to control others with his words, his power to persuade others to do his bid-ding, his uncanny knack for recruiting followers. This "talent" and an inflated sense of his own grandiosity allowed him a sense that any action he might take was justified.

His desire for celebrity status and his delusional mind brought him to expect that he would someday live in a world that he *pos-sessed*, not one that he simply shared. This would not be a socialist world, but one that required his leadership. He bragged about it in a missive to me, providing insight into his self-perceived Godliness:

> *Man, this world is full of unbelievers and I am only a sinner in the*
> *eyes of a world who can't believe so what do I do feel guilty or some-*
> *thing because of the way a world of people who don't understand think I*
> *don't think so but here I am locked away because I frightened people*
> *because no one understands the power of a man like me the power I hold*
> *because truth is reality if it's in song or my guitar or through my word*
> *truth is truth and baby you can't fight the truth you can lock it up but*
> *you can't do away with it.*
>
> Charles Manson, Pelican Bay Prison, 2000

As a reader, it may be clear to you that this is not the product of a healthy or educated mind; but he found and exploited an audience that was less lucid — teenagers hanging out in the Haight Ashbury District of San Francisco, in the "era of love," under the influence of pot, LSD and whatever charismatic personality might stroll by.

Manson put his reformatory years to good use once he was freed: he transferred his tools of manipulation from the cell to the street. He can be charming, when he chooses to be. He lured several people into his lair and into his hidden agenda. And, personally, I can attest that even now he is a master at toying with interviewers, with "the system", and those who research the prison population.

Born in Kentucky in 1934, he was first introduced to reformatory at the age of five, when his mother was arrested for "solicitation" in 1939. It didn't take long for Charles to follow in her illegal ways; he spent his early days on the street, in trouble, usually for petty theft or dealing in drugs. Soon he, too, would become familiar with life behind walls — reform "schools," detention centers and, at times, with no family to go home to, placement with relatives who were strangers to him. He has remarked that he

*"... only knew crime, and when I served time it was no different than the foster care I got on the outside 'cause there was no love for (me) man, no love for a man like me; with a ma like that I had to go make my own love..."*

Charles Manson would someday have love, adoration and a family of his own — and, tragically, murder too.

Manson is like a lot of serial killers: white, male, in his mid-thirties. His profile is that of a man who comes from a negligent background but who is seemingly normal, even persuasive with his kindness toward others and within his community. So, then, if he is no marked exception from the "norm" for serial killers, why single him out for closer consideration?

Charles Manson *is* different in that he manipulated many others to conform to his deviant views and heinous ways — at least a dozen people. This would be less surprising if he seduced them in the name of religion or race — like the Black Panthers, for example — but, because he had no original philosophy, and no overt political platform, in the beginning, it *does* mark a historical novelty. Manson was just another guy, except for his calm, inviting manner, his charisma. Of course, as people were drawn to him, began to listen to him, and ultimately to follow him, he did create a political purpose for his actions. . . and while Manson seems to take pleasure in appearing a bit crazed in his letters, or during television interviews, he was very calculated in taking precautions not to frighten away those who were becoming "family." He was far less the rambling fool, far more the articulate beast when he was on his "mission."

Charles Manson formed his cult of men and women — mostly young people picked up in the hippy Mecca of Haight Ashbury, in the mid-1960s. He was in his early thirties, had learned to play the guitar while serving time in prison, and, with his deep-set brown eyes, poetic words and folk-style music, he was a magnet to the many drugged or simply confused youngsters in the area. They all had one thing in common: they were slightly lost and largely rebellious, deeply alienated by the country's involvement in the Vietnam War. Mostly, these were young people trying to make sense of their own lives by making statements about life in general. They were middleclass and non-threatening to society, for the most part; adolescents struggling to digest a complex reality.

Nevertheless, they all shared a sense of not fitting in, of being black sheep or outcasts in their families. Charles Manson offered, to such persons, a sense of security. He was slightly older, seemed worldly and very sure of his path, and knew his place amidst the wreckage that existed around him. He spoke clearly of world issues and social problems, how to solve the international crisis — the war — and how to create a better way of life: a communal, loving lifestyle, far from the chaos that Western civilization seemed to be visiting upon itself and its global neighbors. Even the Haight was only an illusion, he said. He was persuasive and articulate, with a relatively high IQ (over 125) that enabled him to dominate lesser minds.

He gathered together his family during what has been dubbed the "Summer of Love," enticing them with his words, his accomplishments as a musician and promises of security. Manson moved his "family members" off the streets to a more "wholesome" environment. A large group followed the leader to southern California during the fall of 1967. Together, they would work a piece of land that he knew of; they would grow vegetables and procreate and begin a new world.

He began simply with love; he created a foundation that appeared safe, non-violent and, to the lost souls that were beginning to make up this cult, a new chance to build a family. Manson didn't want to frighten his group; he could bide his time, slowly introducing the political and social agenda that was prompted by his fantasies, gradually transferring his ideologies unto impressionable people who were beginning to view him as their guru.

There is something to be learned by looking at Manson, and at his loyal followers, and by pondering them collectively as a killing team; something to consider when we assess the deadly powers of persuasion. The men and women who ultimately would be deemed some of the most violent killers were only teenaged runaways when they met Manson; fairly average kids looking for relief from the oppression they sensed around them. None had violent histories; their only crime would be following Manson. . . the intensity of love they felt for him — worship, really — is what makes this group different. People have killed in the name of love — or passion — before. But these were not crimes of passion, they were the work of robots. These young people had been brainwashed, or intimidated, or drugged into a belief system that justified killing — by a diminutive man with a bone to pick with society.

And so, the "family" moved south and settled in at Spawn Ranch, which was actually a deserted movie set. Their new home was complete with old houses, tractors and a couple of trucks. Manson had only recently been paroled from McNeil Island Prison (March 21, 1967); it hadn't taken him long to gather a following and begin to create a world that suited him: one that included open sex, drugs, and obedience to his demands as leader. Sometimes he would ask for an evening with someone's girlfriend. Sometimes he would ask a few of the family members to rob for him. And, explaining that the family would be misunderstood, he persuaded them that they needed to be prepared to protect themselves from "the conservatives," which included the "Pigs," or cops. Rifles and handguns and other weaponry were needed. His demands grew, yet few questions were asked. If Manson, who began referring to himself as the second coming of Christ Jesus, thought the family "needed" anything, he would tap one of his faithful cult members, and the task would be completed — be it robbery, sex, or murder.

As Manson observed his growing power, he began to divulge his more bizarre ideologies. The group's days of peace, love and joy were interrupted more and more often with discussions of war and violence. "Jesus" maintained that he saw danger coming; that unless the family took a stance, they faced the disintegration of the human race.

He said that racial wars in the US were inevitable, *and necessary.* The "Charles Manson Calling" was to ensure the eruption. Why? Because in the aftermath of the storm, there would be a clear need for post-revolutionary leaders. Who? Manson and his growing cult. Manson had a plan. His followers would help him fulfill it. The era was proclaimed: "Helter Skelter." It was up to the Manson family to light the fuse that would set off this event. A statement had to be made that could not be ignored. Four would be selected to lead the way — Linda Kasabian, Susan Atkins, Patricia Krenwinkel and Charles Watson. And the chosen four set out for the hills of Holly-wood to strike a match.

In August of 1969, over a 48-hour time span, America was rocked by the murders of some of Hollywood's greatest contempo-rary idols. Throughout the world, people gasped not only at the idea that such famous and beloved people could be murdered, but at the details — no mere gun shots or quick blows to the head, but liter-ally carving with knives, and pseudo-political messages scrawled in the victims' blood. How many killers were there? There had to be many people involved, as in the first episode they had infiltrated a house full of people and murdered them all. America was terrified. Rumors flew. Was it an anti-white group? Were they drug addicts? No one knew — only that they were successful in killing and in evading capture, and that their crimes left plenty of supposed clues.

The first target was the home of film director Roman Polanski and his wife, Sharon Tate, who was eight months pregnant. Manson's three young women and one man broke in, under an instruction to kill the wealthy, eliminate the elite; to terminate the sort of people whose demise was sure to be noticed. In fact, Manson had sent the pack to what he thought was the home of Dennis Wilson's manager/producer. In earlier years, Manson the "guitarist" had cozied up to Wilson, of the Beach Boys, and Wilson had agreed to show of his lyrics to his manager. It so happened that Manson's amateurish musical efforts were rejected. Now Manson thought, ironically, that under cover of a backhanded political message he would get revenge on the unappreciative band manager. But, unbeknownst to his subordinates, they went to work on the home's more recent occupants. The Polanskis had just moved in.

The deaths were to be brutal; and the evidence (knives, clothing) were to be planted in the black ghettos of Los Angeles. A "war" would surely follow. Chaos in the streets would be inevitable as whites retaliated against blacks, and peace would be resumed only through the enlightened leadership of Manson.

The team arrived at the Polanski estate and, after circling the compound, decided that a change of plan was necessary. While her husband was away on business, Sharon Tate had decided to have a party; she was entertaining four guests. The larger-then-expected group threw the murderers off balance, but ultimately they carried out a frenzy of killing.

Steven Parent was murdered in his car in front of the Polanski home. He was shot four times and stabbed for good measure. Abigail Folger and Voytek Frykowski attempted to escape, but were caught in the backyard by the pool. Folger was stabbed 28 times, and Frykowski was bludgeoned across the skull 13 times, then shot twice. Sharon Tate and Jay Sebring were murdered in the home. After being tied up and hung by their necks over a ceiling rafter,

Tate suffered 16 stabbings in the chest and back and Sebring was stabbed seven times and shot once. Then the "family" went to work, leaving a message behind. Dipping their hands in the victims' blood, they daubed gruesome and inscrutable words on doors and walls: "PIG," and "HELTER SKELTER;" the messages meant nothing to detectives in the first stages of investigation.

Then on August 10, 1969, Manson sent more members out on a mission. The home of Leno and Rosemary LaBianca was the target, this time. Manson decided to accompany his followers, and he personally tied up the victims, telling them they wouldn't be hurt. And then Manson left. Charles Watson, Patricia Krenwinkel and Leslie Van Houten were left to finish the job. Rosemary LaBianca was stabbed 41 times. Leno LaBianca was also stabbed at least two dozen times, and then pierced with a knife and fork that were left protruding from his body. The victims' blood was again used as the ink to leave a signature behind.

In an unrelated event, police arrested a group of hippies attempting to dismantle a piece of construction equipment near Spawn Ranch. Susan Atkins, who had participated in the Tate/Polanski killings, was among those arrested. High on a variety of drugs, she babbled to another inmate about her recent exploits. Her story quickly got around the ward. Her cellmates were terrified by her bravado; her bragging was more suitable for a shopping spree than a killing spree. And she named names, including Charles Manson's.

Though it could not be proved that Charles Manson had directly participated in the murders committed at the Polanski residence, in 1970, after a long investigation that brought new meaning to the term "mind control," he was convicted in those and the La Bianca murders.

Susan Atkins, Patricia Krenwinkel and Leslie Van Houten were also found guilty. Manson made a mockery of the crime and the trial, cracking jokes, knocking over benches and calling out obscenities. His "family" would follow his lead, creating havoc in the courtroom. His grip on these people was profound, even during the trial. He was found culpable in the eyes of the law; all the defendants were found guilty and sentenced to death. The sentences were later commuted to life imprisonment when the U.S. Supreme Court abolished the death penalty.

In August 1971, six more members of the Manson cult were arrested after exchanging contraband with police. In an attempt to organize a break out for their leader, they had robbed a gun shop in southern California. Among the group was Mary Brunner, who was further charged with murder, and sentenced to life imprisonment.

While these cases resulted in sentencing against Manson and his followers, many unsolved murders are directly linked to the clan but conclusive evidence is lacking. Among others, the remains of a defense attorney of Manson's, last seen with two "family" members, were found in an isolated area near Sespe Hot Springs, California.

Over a hundred books have been written about the cult, its leader, and the inconceivable actions that can be induced by brainwashing. Charles Manson may not be the most vile criminal in US history, but certainly he is one of the most frightening, and as he'd hoped to be, the most famous.

His followers were a mix of students and young runaways, vulnerable to his influence. Now they wear the stigma of having perpetrated some of the most grisly crimes in the United States. Other "families" have killed more people, and some groups were larger; but Manson has taken particular pleasure in selling the story of his deviant activities, romanticizing his actions and targeting celebrities to elevate his own infamy. For these reasons, he left his mark, and he will — until someone reaches new "heights" of "lowness" — be remembered as one of the world's most maniacal serial killers. This is fine by Charles Manson, as long as he is simply not forgotten, which appears unlikely. And he still styles himself "Jesus Christ" during some interviews today.

In California alone, there are 600 women in prison for killing an abusive husband or lover. While that is a small number compared to the women in prison for credit fraud, petty theft, and other nonviolent crimes, it does represent a significant population. At least 72% of crimes committed by women are crimes of survival (i.e., theft of, or to buy, food, clothing, baby items), or credit card fraud or sexual solicitation.[*]

Many will argue that, statistically, women benefit from judicial lenience in receiving "life sentences" when their male counterparts may be given "death sentences." This discrepancy is, in fact, very often fair. Most women who engage in violent acts, and specifically murder, do so only when driven to it for self preservation or to

---

[*] American Civil Liberties Union, *Women and Prison*, 2001.

protect their children — or, in the kind of murders discussed in this work, when their lovers or someone else with power over them drives them to it. Considering that one partner is the leader and the initiator, and the other is psychologically dependent on him and may be in danger for her own life, indeed one has to wonder whether the sentences imposed on the weaker partner are not, very often, far too harsh rather than too lenient. The psychological phenomenon here is comparable to the battered woman syndrome.

Team killers are couples or groups in which a man (or a woman who has developed the kind of forceful and dominating character more commonly found among a certain type of man, as described earlier in this book), manipulates a weaker partner, often a woman, into becoming a killer. This weaker partner usually has no history of criminal activity, but under his "leadership" she will recruit victims and participate in killing them, at the request of the man.

The male, or lead, killer cunningly targets a certain gentle, passive type of woman and moves in on her, taking advantage of her inclination to please. This type of woman is already intimidated by life, and will cling to a partner she perceives as being strong and able to protect her; of course, she is extremely open to intimidation from him, as well. In other words, once she is involved, it is hard for her to not obey, it is frightening to even imagine displeasing her lover, it is inconceivable to say "no" to any of his whims and demands.

The lead (usually male) killer looks for just such a partner. She is the perfect killer, beneath the "nice" persona. She can't let go of someone she loves; she can't reject him and is terrified that he might leave her. And she is so approachable that she can lure potential victims without ever touching off suspicion. She can be the perfect accomplice in achieving his fantasy.

It is immaterial whether the team killers are homosexual or heterosexual, male or female; what these types of teams have in common (including families or large groups) are the phenomena of passive and aggressive personalities and patterns of (usually) male dominance. Under the leadership of a killer, a vulnerable or passive woman might become a killer alongside him. So might a vulnerable or passive male. So might a woman who falls under the control of a certain type of dominating woman rather than a man: they are all targets for the lover-killer-leader. The weaker partner is lured in and entrapped in someone else's vicious game, yet the courts usually punish her or him as harshly as they punish the initiator of the crimes, regardless of the degree of participation and degree of mental capacity.

If the female, or passive partner, becomes emotionally involved with a (masked) serial killer, it is almost inevitable that she will become a follower/aide, his puppet, used to lure victims. He is masterful and cunning — first acting lovingly with his "woman," then threatening her emotional and/or physical survival, and possibly her children's. She (sometimes he) would do anything to avoid incurring his displeasure.

Are the weaker partners in these scenarios evil? Many of them appear to have been acting out of fear. Do they come to enjoy the killing? They may become desensitized. They may also become dependent on the praise and "love" their participation inspires (even briefly) in the leader. Sometimes they are addicted to drugs, creating delusions and loss of inhibition. Most of these women start out with some level of conscience, but circumstances may evolve so that their empathy toward other beings is erased, as it has been in the team leaders. The "junior partner" comes to see nothing but the need to fulfill his demands, not to fail, and above all else, to survive. How, as Dr. Premiston asks in his Foreword, shall we apportion guilt and establish appropriate legal sanctions? And how, as Jennifer Furio asks in the Introduction, can we protect young children from the many forms of psychological damage that enable people to become killers?

*Urzula Brekhart*
Human Rights Advocate
PARC (Prison Activist Resource Center)
Oakland, California

# REFERENCES

Part I

Rosemary and Frederick West

1. Neil Darbyshire and Paul Stokes, "The Rosemary West Trial: Common Sense Says That West Must Be Guilty," *Electronic Telegraph* (Internet Edition), November 15, 1995.

2. Neil Darbyshire, "Legal Oddities Clinched the Case against West," *The Electronic Telegraph* (Internet edition), November 23, 1995.

3. Sheila Isenberg, *Women Who Love Men Who Kill*. Dell, 1991.

Catherine and David Birnie

1. Brian Lane and Wilfred Gregg, *The Encyclopedia of Serial Killers*, Second Edition. Diamond Books, 1999.

2. "Catherine and David — Essay on Team Crime," *Court TV* (Internet Edition, 2001)

3. R.E. and Lea E. Masters, *Perverse Crimes in History*. New York: Julian Press, 1963

Debra Denise Brown and Alton Coleman

1. Jason Moss, *The Last Victim*. Warner Books, 1999.

2. R.L. Hough, *Thrill Killing*, thesis. Internet Edition, March 1999, based on R.L. Hough, *Profiling the Lust Killer*, Pinnacle, 1996.

3. K. Segrave, *Women Serial and Mass Murderers*, Jefferson, NC: McFarland, 1992.

Cynthia Coffman and James Marlow

1. Sheila Isenberg, *Women Who Love Men Who Kill*. Dell, 1991.

2. David Lester, *Serial Killers, the Insatiable Passion*. Philadelphia: Charles

Press, 1995.

3.  "I'm the Lone Wolf." *San Bernardino News*, San Bernardino, CA, Internet Edition, 1996.

Caril Ann Fugate and Charles Starkweather

1.  Lang and Gregg, *Hunting Humans.* Berkeley Books, May 1995.
2.  Eric W. Hickey, *Serial Murderers and Their Victims.* Belmont, CA.: Wadsworth, 1991.
3.  Kelleher and Kelleher, *Murder Most Rare.* Greenwood Publishers, 1998.

Myra Hindley and Ian Brady

1.  David Millward, "Free Me, Begs Sorrowful Myra Hindley," *(London) Electronic Telegraph* (Internet edition), December 8, 1994.
2.  Schecter and Everitt, *A to Z Encyclopedia of Serial Killers*, New York: Pocket Books, 1996.
3.  Wilson and Wilson, *The Killers Among Us.* New York: Time Warner, 1996.
4.  Jonathan Goodman, Ed., *Celebrated Trials*, Newton Abbot: David and Charles, 1973.

Judith and Alvin Neelley

1.  "Hunting Humans — Alvin and Judith Ann Neelley," Section: "Hunting Humans," in Kozel Multimedia, *Mind of a Killer*, CD-ROM. Chatsworth, CA: Cambrix, 1995.
2.  Grover Maurice Godwin, *Hunting Serial Predators: A Multivariate Classification Approach to Profiling Violent Behavior.* Bantam, 2000.

Carol Bundy and Douglas Clark

1.  *The Sunset Murders*, Lousie Farr, Pocket STAR Books, 1994
2.  David Lester, *Serial Killers: the Insatiable Passion, op. cit.*
3.  "Lust Killers," *Court TV*, Internet Edition, October 14, 1999.

Charlene and Gerald Gallego

1.  Wilson and Wilson, *The Killers Among Us.* New York: Time Warner, 1996.
2.  Ray Biondi and Walt Hecox, *All His Father's Sins.* California: Prima Publishing, 1988.

Martha Beck and Raymond Fernandez

1.  Wenzell Brown, *Introduction to Murder.* London: Dakers, 1953.

2.  Pearl Buck, *The Honeymoon Killers*. London: Sphere Books, 1970.
3.  Robert Ressler, Ann W. Resler and John E. Douglas, *Homicide: Patterns and Motives*. New York: Lexington, 1988.

Karla Homolka and Paul Bernardo
1.  *Court TV* (Internet Edition 2000), www.crimelibrary.com, chap 1-8.
2.  William Roughed, ed., *Notable Trials*. London: Hodge, 1996.
3.  "Karla: Predator or Prey"— *Court TV*, Internet Edition, November, 1997.
4.  "The Trial of Paul Bernardo"— *Court TV*, Internet Edition, November 1997.
5.  D.T. Lunde, *Murder and Madness*. San Francisco: San Francisco Book Company, Second ed. 1996.
6.  G. Sparrow, *Women Who Murder*. New York: Abelard-Chuman, 1970.

Part II
Catherine Wood and Gwendolyn Graham
1.  "Ex-Nursing Home Aide Sentenced in Killings," *Charlotte (North Carolina) Observer* (Internet Edition), October 12, 1989.

Annie Waters and Amelia Sach

1.  "Hunting Humans — Amelia Sach and Annie Waters," in Kozel Multimedia, Section: "Hunting Humans,"*Mind of a Killer*, CD-ROM. Chatsworth, CA.: Cambrix, 1995.
2.  Archie Combs, *Baby Farms, Infanticide*. Pocket Books, 1981.

Part III
Dean Corll and Elmer Wayne Henley
1.  Jack Olsen, *The Man with the Candy*. New York: Talmy Franklin, 1975.
2.  John K. Gurwell, *Mass Murder in Houston*. Houston: Cordovan Press, 1974.
3.  Wilson and Seaman, *American Serial Murderers*. New American Library, second edition, 1982.

Lawrence Bittaker and Roy Norris
1.  Ronald Marman and Dominic Bosco, *Alone with the Devil*. Second Edition. New York: Doubleday, 1989.
2.  Brian Lane and Wilfred Gregg, *The Encyclopedia of Serial Killers*. Berkeley Books, 1995.

3. John Douglas, *MindHunter*. New American Library, 1997.

The Hillside Stranglers
1. Sheila Isenberg, *Women Who Love Men Who Kill*. Dell, 1991.
2. Ted Schwartz, *The Hillside Strangler*. New York: Doubleday, 1985.
3. Darcy O'Brien, *Two of a Kind*. New York: New American Library, 1985

David Gore and Fred Waterfield
1. *Court TV* — Internet Edition 2000, www.crimelibrary.com, Chapters 1-4.
2. Jennifer Furio, *Serial Killer Letters: A Penetrating Look Inside the Minds of Murderers*, Philadelpha: Charles Press, 1998.
3. "Team Killers," *Detective Magazine*, January, 1996 (Internet Access)
4. Dr. Roy Norris, *Profiles in Murder*. New York: Viking, 1988.

Part IV
Zebra Killings
1. Clark Howard, *The Zebra Killings*. London: New English Library [n.d.].

The Chicago Rippers
1. Russel Vorpagel, Joseph Harrington, *Profiles in Murder: An FBI Legend Dissects Killers and Their Crimes*. Berkeley, November 1998.
2. Hickey, *Group Killers"* New York: New York University Press, 1991.
3. Robert D. Koppel, *Signature Killers*. Pocket, 1989

Lainz Hospital
1. Stephen J. Giannangelo, *The Psychopathology of Serial Murder*. Kensington, October 1998.
2. E. Leyton, *Compulsive Killers*. New York: New York University Press, 1986.
3. Thomas E. Gaddis and James O. Long, *Killer*. New York: Macmillan, 1970.
4. R.R. McDonald, *Black Widow*. New York: St. Martin's Press, 1986.

Charles Manson
1. *Parole Hearing Minutes: Charles Manson (1992)*. State of California Board of Prison Terms, April 22, 1992
2. David Lester, *Serial Killing, the Insatiable Passion*. Philadelphia: Charles Press, 1995.
3. Lang and Gregg, *Hunting Humans*. Berkeley Books, May 1995.
4. Jenkins, P. "A Murder 'Wave'?" *Criminal Justice Review* 17 (1): 1-19, 1992.

## Acknowledgements

I especially want to thank my husband, my parents and my children for accepting my need to understand violence within our culture. And while it's difficult for many to fathom my interest in murderers, a growing number of authors and interviewers have encouraged my efforts. Most of all, I want to thank Andrea Secara, my editor, for her support.